WORK

A Teacher's Observations on Composition

WORKING PAPERS:

A Teacher's Observations on Composition

A. M. Tibbetts

University of Illinois at Urbana-Champaign

Scott, Foresman and Company

Glenview, Illinois
Dallas, Texas   Oakland, New Jersey   Palo Alto, California
Tucker, Georgia   London, England

CREDIT LINES

Library of Congress Cataloging in Publication Data

Tibbetts, A. M.
  Working papers.

  Includes bibliographical references.
  1. Rhetoric—Study and teaching. I. Title.
PE1404.T5   808'.042   81-14403
ISBN 0-673-15490-4   AACR2

ACKNOWLEDGMENTS

I teach in a university devoted to footnotes and the higher reaches of scholarship. So you may wonder why I don't have a long list of sources on my writing topics. There are two reasons: the list would be too short, or it would be too long. I once produced an incomplete list for graduate students that ran nine typewritten pages, single-spaced. Once you start making such a list, it seems impossible to stop. If you include Aristotle, why not George Campbell? If you mention Mina Shaughnessy, why not Linda Flower?

For anyone who knows the scholarship on composition, any names I might put here would be superfluous. For anyone who doesn't, here is a good place to start: *Teaching Composition: Ten Bibliographical Essays*, ed. Gary Tate, Texas Christian University Press, 1976.

I would like to thank the publishers and authors listed on the copyright page for permission to reprint their selections. I am also grateful to Scott, Foresman and Company for allowing me to use some material from the 1974 edition of *Strategies of Rhetoric*, and my thanks to the National Council of Teachers of English for permission to use parts of my article, "Rhetorical Stance Revisited," *CCC Journal*, October 1975.

I also would like to acknowledge these persons who read and criticized the manuscript: William Gibson, Idaho State University; Eugene Hammond, University of Maryland; James A. Parrish, Jr., University of South Florida; John J. Ruszkiewicz, University of Texas; Joyce S. Steward, University of Wisconsin; Joseph M. Williams, University of Chicago. Of course, these scholars are not responsible for errors of fact or judgment in the book.

A.M.T.

Give me the murky month of February, with snow blowing on the windowpane of the classroom, the early darkness falling and the gaslight bright in the classroom. That and a blackboard, and a theorem, and a professor — the right kind, absorbed, ecstatic and a little silly. — Stephen Leacock

To Charlene

CONTENTS

Introduction

We don't pay enough attention to the "ordinary," successful writer: to how he thinks, how he approaches problems, how he solves them—how, even, he tries to avoid them in the first place.

These essays do not represent a new theoretical statement on composition or teaching. They are not written for the specialist, scholar, or system-maker. That I have drawn heavily on the knowledge of these valuable persons will be evident if they should be so incautious as to peer inside the book. I have chosen to write for a different audience—the "new" teachers of composition (not to mention certain new writers), who often have little more than a textbook to guide them. And textbooks have their built-in limitations. I know this as a writer of them.

The epigraph above was a note to myself in 1970 when I started on these essays. For more than ten years, they have been written and rewritten as "working papers" for my composition courses and activity as a consultant in writing. Each paper had a title "The *Problem* of _____," the idea being that I would try to isolate the major problems that writers (and student-writers) have and keep a private diary-essay of possible solutions. I was interested in rhetorical applications—how do compositions, or parts of them, tend to work? And also—how can certain strategies of writing and teaching make a difference in a particular composition?

Some of these "strategies" are discussed in textbooks, some are not. Some that are in textbooks seem to be more useful when they are called by different names or handled somewhat differently. I have found, for example, that students benefit from a discussion of how well-made arguments tend to *reveal* and *pace* themselves. This, added to standard textbook material, helps the student control the argument he is writing—whether he is a freshman, a graduate student in English, a chemist writing a technical paper, or a company vice-president preparing an end-of-year production statement.

Last year, I gathered the working papers that appeared to be most relevant and rewrote them for this small book, which is designed to complement the teacher's (or writer's) strategic weapons. I assume that the teacher and writer are usually the same person. That is, the teacher also writes; the writer—no matter who he is or where he works—is always teaching himself and learning. You can't write a paragraph without learning something, however little.

Why did I choose the five papers published here? Because, as I worked with writers, five problems presented themselves most often—those of readability, "grammar," stance, organization, and argument. For example, an unreadable sentence may have one or more causes—weak stance, faulty choice of grammatical subject, the writer's unwillingness to come to grips with the point of his argument, an organizational weakness a few lines earlier. If we ask the right questions about the bad sentence, the writer may be able to solve his problem himself. And, given sufficient practice, to solve other problems in writing as they present themselves.

These papers represent *observations:* somewhat disunified and incomplete attempts to say a few things about the work that we all do, about the difficulties that we who write and teach all face. They are rhetorical artifacts of a professional struggle.

The order of the papers is not that in which they were written, nor that in which I teach the material as units. In any writing course of mine—whether directed to freshmen, graduate students, or businessmen—I teach *stance* first. But on the advice of the person to whom the papers are dedicated, I have arranged them in what she calls their "most readable order."*

*My daily work with students has always required samples of good and bad writing for discussion. Some of the samples reproduced here are rather long. I tried placing some of the longer ones at the back of an essay, but readers of the manuscript objected that they did not like to flip pages back and forth. So I have inserted all samples in the text.

1 Teaching the Readable Sentence*

. . . to establish relative readability as our common stylistic goal in teaching composition.
E. D. Hirsch, Jr., *The Philosophy of Composition*[1]

Teachers have long noted that if students cannot create reasonably clear sentences, they will not succeed as writers. On the other hand if they can consistently make such sentences, the other blocks to writing can often be removed.

We are not much concerned here about theories of readability, although they have their uses; nor with detailed grammatical analyses of the readable sentence—although handling grammatical operations properly is necessary if the writer is to succeed. Rather, we are concerned with the sentence as *perceived* by student as writer and by teacher as editor. Let us face the hard reality of our peculiar situation. Teacher and student ordinarily perceive the sentence very differently, much as my mechanic and I perceive my car. To me, the damned contraption is a miserable mystery. I know it sometimes runs and sometimes doesn't, but have no idea why in either case. The mechanic knows (I think), but he can't tell me in terms I can understand or use to make the thing run myself.

*This essay is meant to be read with the next one, on teaching grammar.

We need a system of teaching the readable sentence which helps to create a single perception that is shared by both teacher and student. They should share a few simple premises, definitions, strategies of composing, and devices of editing. Where all these come from—whether from grammar, psychology, rhetoric, intuition, editorial practice, or systems of pedagogy—is of relatively little consequence.

PREMISES

I teach "readability" to different kinds of people—ranging from college freshmen, to graduate students in English, to businessmen interested in improving communication for the sake of profit. Of every audience I always ask this question: *What is the most important thing about the English sentence?* Typical answers: It has a subject and verb. It must be logical. It must have at least one complete idea. Etc. No one ever gives the answer I am after: the most important thing about the sentence—the first premise in teaching readability—is *that it is read from left to right.* What seems like a trivial accident in the history of transcribing speech is to the modern writer of English a starting point. Where do sentences often go wrong? On the left, where they begin.

Consider this corollary to Murphy's Law: *If readers can misread a sentence, they will.* Almost anything—from a poorly chosen word to a piece of ambiguous logic—will derail them. And derailment typically occurs early, near the left of the sentence. If you can get your readers past the subject and verb of the main clause, you have a much better chance of pulling them through the rest of the sentence without mishap. We should concentrate on beginning a sentence properly.

In his master's thesis, a student writes: *The specialized mechanics [design and construction] of other equipment types are not capable of these operations.* He has begun wrong. He means, as it turns out: *Other types of equipment cannot perform these operations.* A forty-year-old union executive writes: *One of the most important reasons for supporting the union is stable employment.* By starting his sentence with greater precision, he makes it clearer: *Workers who want stable employment should join the union.* Obviously, issues of *stance* (see Chapter 3) are involved in such editorial decisions, whether they are made by teacher or student. For that matter, editorial decisions tend to involve simultaneously many techniques and problems of writing—one reason why teaching composition is so charmingly difficult.

A second premise arises out of the first: the readable sentence tends to be predictable. In fact, "relative predictability" may be a major indicator of the readable sentence. This point Professor Hirsch makes often in *The Philosophy of Composition*. The readable sentence fulfills expectations that are both syntactic and semantic. Mary Hiatt gives an example of predictable relationships:

> In language, the probabilities are governed to a greater or lesser extent by the preceding choices. For example, if the first word in a sequence is *due*, there are many words that can follow. If the second word is *to*, the range of possibilities for the third word is still wide, as it is if the third word is *the*. But if the fourth word is *fact*, the possibilities for the fifth word are much more limited, and therefore its predictability is much higher than that of any of the preceding words. The fifth word will almost certainly be *that;* it almost certainly will *not* be *umbrella*.[2]

To dramatize the notion of predictability, I have asked students to read good and bad sentences slowly word by word, covering the unread portion with a piece of paper. They can often tell early in the sentence whether it is going to be readable. Professor Hiatt commented on the very low predictability of her sample of scientific prose. One example of hers is this sentence: *Successive 1-ml fractions were then drawn off with a hypodermic syringe, starting at the top of the tube, and tested for agglutin activity.*[3]

Students find this unreadable, and not just because of its subject matter. One can rewrite it for much greater predictability: *Starting at the top of the tube, I then drew off successive 1-ml fractions with a hypodermic syringe and tested them for agglutin activity.*

A third premise involves the relation between writing and speaking. Now and again writers should be required to "talk out" a few sentences, and then to write down what they say. All papers—with no exception—should be read aloud before they are turned over to teachers or other readers. The ear catches what the mind misses. Too, the life of the sentence is perhaps more in the ear than in the eye. "Everybody writes prose for the eye nowadays, and it's quite dead." So said Logan Pearsall Smith, who is quoted by the philosopher Brand Blanshard in his discussion of the importance of rhythm. Blanshard continues:

> ... rhythm has been anything but a small concern to the masters of English prose. They plainly meant us to hear what they wrote. ... For rhythm is one of the subtlest of all instruments in the delicate work of conveying thought. But there is one general rule that is at once so simple and so near the heart of the whole matter, that I must at least mention it.
>
> This rule is to make the emphases of sense and rhythm coincide. Plain men know by a sort of instinct where to hit hard; they never say, "There is in my mind a desire which would be gratified if you were to transfer the hammer into my possession"; they say, "Give me the hammer." This is true style. Someone has said, "All peasants have style," and philosophers cannot afford to get wholly out of touch with the fine economy of natural talk.[4]

Such "natural talk" is more and more missing from American prose. There are several causes. One is the influence of bureaucratic cant, pseudo-scientific language, and professional jargons of many kinds. Perhaps the most significant cause is the fear we Americans have of sounding unserious. What Sheridan Baker has called "the tone of intelligent and agreeable conversation"[5] in writing is not enough for us. We want something weightier, more German-sounding and glamourous.

Indeed *glamour*—which has its roots in mystery, magic, and (of all things) the word *grammar*—is an excellent word to associate with readability. But *glamour* also implies the use of speech. The incantations of both grammarians and magicians have certain similarities, not the least of which is their power to inculcate belief and knowledge. One remembers the old oral classroom drills in Latin, Greek, and English: out of the mist of time echoes an alluring and antiphonal pedagogy.

FAMILIAR WORDS

The great physician and teacher Sir William Osler wrote in the *Principles and Practice of Medicine:*

> We know but little of the incubation period in acute lobar pneumonia. It is probably very short. There are sometimes slight catarrhal symptoms for a day or two. As a rule, the disease sets in abruptly with a severe chill, which lasts from fifteen to thirty minutes or longer. In no acute disease is an initial chill so constant or so severe. The patient may be taken abruptly in the midst of his work, or may awaken out of a sound sleep in a rigor. The temperature taken during the chill shows that the fever has already begun. If seen shortly after the onset, the patient has usually features of an acute fever, and complains of headache and general pains.

On the same subject, another (unidentified) physician wrote:

> Symptomatology relative to impending or incipient onset of illness generally manifests itself initially via a marked chill, following which a rapid rise of temperature to the 103°-105° range is characteristically observed. Cutaneous palpation demonstrates evidence of considerable warmth and dryness, while erythema of the malar eminences accompanies fever in a majority of instances. The facies is furthermore characterized by an expression of anxiety, with alar flaring occurring synchronously with inspiratory activity. There are usually also cephalgia, myalgia, severe thirst, marked anorexia and other constitutional manifestations commonly attendant upon any febrile condition, as well as tachycardia, with pulse substantially higher than 100, and tachypnea with respiratory frequency exceeding sometimes 60 per minute.[6]

The two passages are different in several ways, the most distinctive perhaps being in word choice. The second writer derails his reader with a barrage of two-dollar words. By contrast, except for the name of the disease being described and two words (*catarrhal* and *rigor*), Sir William uses words found in the vocabulary of ordinary educated readers. Dr. John Dirckx, a practicing physician, in his comment on the two passages calls the second one "rubbish."[7]

My students are full of rubbish, although not of the technical kind just seen. Typically, they will write of how something *functions* instead of how it *works*. And they will start a sentence: *Determination of sorority membership is made by* . . . instead of: *Ten girls form the most powerful voting bloc in* . . . (that is what the writer meant to say).

Everybody in our business talks about the short word being better than the long one. I'm not sure about this. Other things being equal, perhaps the main issue is not the length of a word but its genuine familiarity. Why *genuine?* Many words, particularly those presently in vogue or in some way faddish, are familiar more as noises than as representations of exact meaning. When *detente* was in every headline, I asked many educated people what it meant. Almost no one knew. Later I asked ten people who worked professionally with language what the familiar term *passive voice* meant. The only person who came close was our departmental secretary. On thousands of highway signs you'll find the expression *trauma center.* I asked twenty educated Americans what that meant, and no one knew for certain although four made good guesses.

THE "UNIT RULE"

Recently, I was lucky enough to teach one of the best students I've ever seen. He was good at everything, from impromptu speaking to grammatical analysis. He wrote very well. A third-year law student, he was also an intern in a large Chicago law firm. As part of our course work, he revised a legal paper he had written. Here is part of his revision:

> Police had arrested Chadwick and his companions at a Boston train station for possession of marijuana. After incarcerating the suspects at the federal building, the police searched a foot-locker which Chadwick had been carrying. Significantly, the search—which occurred at the federal building—was conducted

one and one-half hours after the arrest. The police did not have a warrant allowing the search. At his trial, Chadwick challenged the admissability (into evidence) of the marijuana found in the footlocker, claiming that the search violated the fourth amendment. The district court, agreeing that the search was unreasonable, suppressed the evidence. On appeal, the First Circuit affirmed. After losing at the district and circuit courts, the government appealed to the Supreme Court. But once again, the government lost; the Supreme Court affirmed. Balancing Chadwick's interest in the privacy of his footlocker against the need for an immediate, warrantless search, the Court found the search unreasonable. In the course of its opinion, the Court considered and rejected the government's attempt to create a new exception to the warrant requirement, one which would allow police to search moveable containers without first obtaining a warrant. Additionally, the Court held that the search was not properly incident to Chadwick's arrest.

This writing is highly readable—and also "legal." That is, lawyers could not complain that it is unacceptable in legal definition or practice. We all know that legal writing is often bad—awful, so far as laymen are concerned. Lawyers like to claim that their profession requires verbal complexity and exact jargon. This is seldom, if ever, true. Here is a translation of some lawyerly rubbish—the translation is as legal as the original.

From the old and new Master Charge agreements of the First National Bank of Boston:

Old Agreement

Cardholder and any other person applying for, using or signing the Card promise, jointly and severally, to pay the Bank the principal of all loans plus, as provided in paragraph 4. FINANCE CHARGES. Payments shall be made each month at Bank or as Bank may direct, on or before the Payment Due Date, in the amount of (a) the greater of $10 or an amount equal to 1/36th of the Total Debit Balance not in excess of the Maximum Credit on the related Statement Date plus (b) any amounts owing and delinquent plus (c) any excess of the Total Debit Balance over the Maximum Credit.

New Agreement

Although you may pay back more, you must pay us a monthly Minimum Payment. This monthly Minimum Payment will be 2.7% of the new balance plus any amounts past due, but at least $10. If the new balance is less than $10, the Minimum Payment will be the entire balance. The new balance will include the outstanding amounts that you have borrowed, plus a *finance charge.*[8]

The rewritten example of good legal prose follows what I have called the "unit rule." The rule identifies four units of meaning in the sentence:[9]

Units = *sentence base, opener, interrupter, closer.*

1. _____opener_____ , _____BASE_____ .

   Example: During her nurse's training, she seemed very happy.

2. ___BASE___ , interrupter , __BASE (continued)__ .

   Example: My doctor's fees, designed especially for poverty patients, were lower than I had expected.

3. _____BASE_____ , _____closer_____ .

   Example: The owners said nothing about trading their aging quarterback, probably because the team thought of him as their leader.

Some observations about *units of meaning:*

1. There are two kinds of units—*base* and *free* (openers, interrupters, closers).
2. The *sentence base* is an independent unit of meaning, capable of standing by itself.
3. *Free units* are almost always dependent, and cannot stand by themselves. They may be single words, phrases, or subordinate clauses.
4. A unit is both grammatical and rhetorical.
5. The boundaries of the unit are marked by punctuation— period, comma, dash, parentheses. But since punctuation is not a science writers do not always mark boundaries

consistently—as I did not put a comma after the opening clause in this sentence.

It is useful to watch an experienced editor work on prose to make it more readable. He will take a sentence like this: *There have been no flu deaths from even the more virulent types of the disease for the past ten years in the county.* And break it into several units, one base and two free: *For the past ten years, there have been no flu deaths in the county—not even from the most virulent types of the disease.* Editors do such work instinctively; few of them have a theory of readability. But it is clear that in their *practice* they are trying:

1. To break up the sentence into clearly recognizable units of meaning;
2. To shorten the units (the original sentence was one unit of 23 words);
3. To make the grammatical units correspond with the rhetorical units;
4. To create strong emphases where they had not existed.

These four elements of readability form the "unit rule." Students have found the rule helpful for several reasons. It provides a *shape* for the sentence, something that they can visualize easily. Diagraming a sentence on a blackboard is simple and quick. A free unit is a straight line drawn with chalk; a base is drawn with the chalk laid on its side:

Two openers and a base:

―――――――――――― , ―――――――――――― , ▬▬▬▬▬▬▬▬▬ .

A base and interrupter:

▬▬▬▬▬▬▬▬ , ―――――――――― , ▬▬▬▬▬▬▬▬▬ .

A base, interrupter, and two closers:

▬▬▬▬▬ (――――――) ▬▬▬▬ — ―――――― , ―――――――― .

Visualizing sentence structure seems to be a great help to all writers in trouble, at whatever level. My thirty-year-old graduate students benefit from a combination of analysis and diagraming as much as freshmen do.

The unit rule gives students choices to make and a place to put things. Before learning it, they tend to compose by throwing words at the page. After learning it, they have both terms and strategies available: "Break the sentence into units, and put these words up front in an opener." At this writing, I have fifteen graduate students—none from the English Department—in a graduate composition course who are writing more readable prose after only two sessions on the rule. The idea of sentence units was totally new to them.

Punctuation, a problem even for mature students, is easier to manage using the rule because the units are delimited by the common marks.

The unit rule is a good tool for analyzing certain pieces of writing. Bad prose usually violates it. Good prose—such as that written by Sir William Osler and my law student—tends to follow it. Note these sentences of the young lawyer's:

Police had arrested Chadwick and his companions at a Boston train station for possession of marijuana.

_____ .

After incarcerating the suspects at the federal building, the police searched a footlocker which Chadwick had been carrying.

_____, _____ .

Significantly, the search—which occurred at the federal building—was conducted one and one-half hours after the arrest.

_____, _____ — _____ — _____ .

The police did not have a warrant allowing the search.

_____ .

At his trial, Chadwick challenged the admissability (into evidence) of the marijuana found in the footlocker, claiming that the search violated the fourth amendment.

_____, _____(_____) _____, _____ .

The district court, agreeing that the search was unreasonable, suppressed the evidence.

_____, _____, _____ .

SENTENCE SIGNALS

To return to one of the premises of this essay: the English sentence is one-dimensional; you read it along a straight line. It is for this reason that *sentence signals*—Professor Hirsch calls them *proleptic devices*—become so important in standard prose. Typical signals are *after, because, since, when, before, but, yet*, etc. Such words join the elements of grammar, logic, and rhetoric to provide "pointers" that say, in effect, "The sentence you are about to read will be of a certain kind; it will deal with similarity, cause, time, antithesis, etc." To do its work, the signal must be placed early in its sentence or unit of meaning.

> One signal: *After* sharpening the blade, turn the mower right side up. . . .
> Two signals: "Napoleon loved only himself, *but unlike* Hitler he hated nobody." (J. Christopher Herald)

Consider the signals in this passage, written by Winston Churchill:

> *But* he must have been a difficult man to please. He did not like the Czar, *so* he murdered him and his family. He did not like the Imperial Government, *so* he blew it up. He did not like the Liberalism of Guchkov and Miliukov, *so* he overthrew them. He could not endure the Social Revolutionary moderation of Kerensky and Savinkov, *so* he seized their places. *And when* at last the Communist regime for which he had striven with might and main was established throughout the whole of Russia, *when* the Dictatorship of the Proletariat was supreme, *when* the New Order of Society had passed from visions into reality, *when* the hateful culture and traditions of the individualist period had been eradicated, *when* the Secret Police had become the servants of the Third International, *when* in a word his Utopia had been achieved, he was still discontented. He still fumed, growled, snarled, bit, and plotted.[10]

George Bernard Shaw was one of the few famous writers who said much about signals. In a letter to Sir Cedric Hardwicke, leading actor in one of his plays, Shaw wrote:

My dear Cedric,

You have had such a splendid press that I must hasten to assure you that you came within half an inch of wrecking the play last Monday night on a point, not of acting, but of elementary technique. You tried the extraordinary experiment of delivering your big speech, and a good deal of the rest of the play, without a single article, definite or indefinite, a single preposition, a single conjunction: in short, without any grammatical structure except an occasional interjection and a precarious supply of verbs. There was not a solitary BUT from one end to the other; yet "but" is the most important conjunction in the English language. . . . It is a tragic thing to see you wrecking a great career by despising words of less than three syllables, and shortening the three into two. . . .

Take care of your *buts* and *thoughs* and *fors* and first syllables at the beginnings of the sentences and definite and indefinite articles, and a great career is within your grasp. Neglect them; and your doom will be obscurity, poverty, ruin, despair, disgrace, and damnation. . . .[11]

PREDICATION

Of the major grammatical operations, two stand out as being particularly important in the readable sentence—*predication* and *coordination*.

As defined here, *predication*, (*praedicáre*, "to proclaim or state") is the act of making a statement by marrying a noun and a verb.

Fitzgerald: The rich are different from us.
Hemingway: Yes, they have more money.

The predications are:

rich ⟵⟶ *are*
they ⟵⟶ *have*

Predication, as used here, refers only to that relationship between subject and verb, not to any of the material that follows the verb. The term *predicate*, as it is used in textbooks, is next to useless for the writer. In many complicated sentences you cannot determine with any certainty what the predicate is. Indeed if you want to discuss the grammatical units that follow the subject and verb, you will learn more if you deal with specifics; for example, complements, objects, modifiers.

The predication symbol (S ←——→ V), with its two-way arrow, reminds us that predicating works in two directions. It requires interaction of two grammatical functions: *naming* and *stating*. The noun subject cannot do its job without the verb that is acting with it; the verb is useless without its own subject to act with. Predication is the heart of the sentence. The writer can struggle along without some of the other elements of structure mentioned in this discussion, but unless he can make predications he can say little, except in cryptic fragments:

Sunrise over Iowa
Red roses in bloom
Took arms quickly from sleeves

Writers use four broad kinds of predication to make statements:

1. **Action:**
   I sold them a house.
   They are moving in the right direction.
2. **Is** (uses a **be** or some other linking form):
   What you see is what you get.
   She might have been happy.
   The *cow seems* contented.
3. **Passive:**
   The *bill was paid* by her.
   The *murder was done.*
4. **Expletive:**
   It's a fine *day.*
   There *are* no *months* like May.

In general, a writer employs one kind of predication over another when it fits better what he wants to say. Over the past dozen years, I have made a few rough counts of the predications in samples of running prose written by professionals. In every sample of over a thousand words, *action* and *is* predications have predominated. Yet in very brief samples, the *passive* (and even the *expletive*) can predominate. For instance, one will often find the expletive in narratives and in introductory material. The passive is useful for a number of constructions, one of the commonest being shown in this example: *His fine was paid by a woman who refused to identify herself.* Here the agent *(woman)* is delayed so that the following adjective clause can be placed neatly next to the noun it modifies.

In making sentences more readable, the first *base predication* seems to be most important. Such predications must stand out in the welter of lexical and syntactic coding systems represented in fairly complex sentences.

Here are two examples of editing for readability:

Bad Sentence:	The conclusion of this writer in the final analysis is that the basic question of the controversy is on who or what authority should the sale of marijuana be allowed. (one unit, predication is separated: *conclusion . . . is*)
Edited Sentence:	I conclude that the controversy hinges on one question: who should have the authority to allow the sale of marijuana? (two units, first base predication is unseparated: *I conclude*)
Bad Sentence:	Parental endeavors in regard to education suggest an ambitious drive toward self-improvement and an interest in upward mobility. (one unit, predication is separated: *endeavors suggest*)
Edited Sentence:	A parent may want his children to stay in school for both economic and social reasons: college graduates make more money and live better. (two base units, predications are unseparated: *parent may want; graduates make* and *live*)

Predication should stand out clearly near the front of the sentence base:

Bad Predication:	The government's *investigation* into the shipment of wheat by the exporter *was met* by his refusal in regard to an examination of his method of payments for its domestic transportation.
Better Predication:	The *government investigated* the shipment of wheat by the exporter. . . . But *he blocked* the investigation by refusing to . . . .
Bad Predication:	The *causes* of the mutation of the genes *received* analysis from the scientists.
Better Predication:	The *scientists analyzed* the causes of the mutation of the genes.[12]

These and other examples illustrate how important good predication is in releasing the syntactic energies of a sentence. If a writer starts wrong—with predication that is vague, abstract, or unnecessarily "separated"—he often stumbles into one blunder after another. By contrast, if he is lucky enough to get his predication right, the other parts of the sentence may fall into place.

By definition all clauses have predication. Their number per sentence is limited only by the writer's ingenuity and the reader's patience. Robert Penn Warren writes in the story, "Blackberry Winter": *"When you are nine, you know that there are things that you don't know, but you know that when you know something you know it."*

The sentence has seven predications, and some of the clauses represented interlock in a surprisingly complex way. Yet the sentence is easily read, partly because it is broken into three clear units by the punctuation, and partly because the base predication after the opener is clear and simple.

COORDINATION

Coordination is the grammatical operation of compounding, balancing, paralleling. It's too bad that we have so many terms for what amounts to the same thing. Coordination, which Sheridan Baker somewhere calls "the masonry of syntax," is second only to predication in importance—perhaps because there is so much of it in English prose.

After analyzing the Brown University Million-Word Corpus, Mary Hiatt expressed surprise at the high number of parallelisms:

> To find evidence that approximately 50 percent of English sentences contain some sort of parallelism was quite unexpected. Parallelism, it seemed, was everywhere. Presumably, 50 percent of the sentences that writers—teachers, students, and scholars—produce may contain parallelism, "faulty" or otherwise.[13]

Professor Hiatt goes on to remark that the figure of 50 percent may be too low:

> Consider, for example, the following sentence:
>> If presidents, deans, trustees, and regents are unwilling or unable to protect and exalt the dignity of the university, they should be grateful to students who have remembered it and exalted it.
>
> In the gross signal program, the four parallel constructions would count only as one, since the computer would find and print out the sentence on the basis of any one of the signals.
>
> Multiple parallelisms in a sentence may occur *seriatim*, as in the cited sentence, or they may be embedded, where one parallelism, usually a doublet, is part of a "larger" parallel structure, as in "The largest and newest bank and the old post office stood side by side." The parallel adjectives *largest* and *newest* can be said to be embedded in the first element or member of the compound subject, which comprises parallel nominals with the head words, *bank* and *post office*. In the gross signal program, embedded parallelisms would also not be reported.
>
> Further, this program did not report the occurrence of asyndeton, series following colons, and independent clauses joined by a semicolon, or those parallelisms that would have been detected by the "quasi-signals."
>
> Indication of this much parallelism in our written language had unexpected stylistic implications.[14]

Certainly parallelism—or *coordination*, as I'm calling it here—

has implications for readability. Yet, typically, writers do not have a working knowledge of a device that probably appears in more than half their own sentences. If they know about coordination at all, they remember it in connection with rules about "faulty parallelism" in textbooks. They are not accustomed to thinking of coordination as a positive aspect of syntax. Because the rhetoric of the sentence requires vast numbers of doublets and triplets—along with not a few series—students need to practice writing them. Several things are involved: logic, sentence structure, and rhythm. Generally, the firmer the rhythm and the clearer the coordinating pattern, the more readable the prose.

Weak coordination often goes hand in hand with faulty predication. In the edited versions, predications are italicized; coordinated elements are underlined:

Weak: The quality of a comic strip exists in relation to the drawings, the language as well as the situations involved.

Edited: A *comic strip is* only as good as its drawings, dialogue, and situations.

Weak: Also clear in the activity between the students in the Senate are their wish for clarifying pass-fail, the need for better discipline procedures, and for watering the plant of faculty-student relationships.

Edited: *Students* in the Senate *want to clarify* the pass-fail option, *create* better procedures for discipline, and *improve* faculty-student relationships generally.

Weak: None of the principal uses of the Freudian method in personality analysis are the determination of personality defects and utilization of their cures.

Edited: When they analyze personality, *Freudians* ordinarily *do* not *wish* to determine defects or suggest cures.

Weak: It is the exploration of student differences in response to the teacher's stimulus questions which cause the student to return to the text seeking justification for their opinions and that ultimately encourages the articulation of their personal views.

Edited: After responding to the teacher's questions, the *stu-*

dents will return to the text—first, to justify their opinions and, second, to organize their own views on the subject.

The weak sentences were taken from printed sources, and the edited versions appeared to be reasonably clear and logical in context.

NOUN DISEASE

The other day, I was editing a paper written for my graduate course in composition. The writer was a forty-year-old economist. I was performing the usual cutting and sewing necessary in editorial surgery when something appeared that made me pause in the operation. A few minutes later I closed the patient and pronounced him incurable—in my own mind, at any rate. At his age the dread disease I had found—*nounitis*—is usually fatal. Even in young, lively writers nounitis can move quickly through the syntactical system until the flow of ideas to the brain is permanently impaired. Unfortunately, the patient often keeps on living, producing comatose sentences for many years.

What I had seen in the guts of the economist's paper were these cancers in two sentences: *ramification potentials, resource use; attitude myopia.*

The linguist calls these *noun strings.* Noun strings, as an article in *Fine Print*—the newsletter of the Document Design Center—points out, "are everywhere in our written and spoken language":

Doublets are especially common and well-accepted: *day care, form letter, pressure cooker, case study, career choice, grant application, life style.* Strings of three or more nouns are not common in everyday speech or writing, but are very common in professional jargon: *health service provider, management information requirement, system level specification, Document Design Center, human factors engineering support, video training system application, U.S. Army weapons systems.* These all may seem reasonable and familiar to you, even if you don't know exactly what they mean. But excesses are also quite common, particularly in the Federal government: just what exactly is a *host area crisis shelter production planning workbook?*[15]

As *Fine Print* remarks, the problem with many noun strings is that we don't know what they mean. Ten years ago, Bruce Price encountered the title of a book, *Reality Therapy*. He asked: "Do you gather that the author uses reality as a means of therapy or that the goal of his treatment is facing reality or that he has worked out some sort of therapy which he applies to reality?" Price called *nounitis* a "modifier noun proliferation increase phenomenon" and suggested a campaign against it.[16]

Fine Print rightly says that many noun strings need to be "unpacked": "We can rewrite them as prepositional phrases and relative clauses." The suggestion is a good one, assuming that you and the writer (or student) can discover the meaning that lurks in the particular string. Here are typical changes the writers and I have agreed upon:

Original: In the early adolescence enrichment program, . . .

Edited: In the program of enrichment we designed for thirteen-year-olds, . . .

Original: When facility termination occurred . . . .

Edited: When the Congress ordered that the base be closed . . . .

Original: . . . after which there will be a consumer liquidity squeeze.

Edited: . . . after which the consumer will have less money to spend.

Original: . . . monetary policy assumption . . . .

Edited: We assume that this policy of spending more money than we have will increase inflation.

Original: . . . transverse wave propagation analysis . . . .

Edited: . . . after they analyzed the propagation of the transverse waves, . . .

"WHO DOES WHAT?"

Many years ago I heard about the *who does what* trick from a friend who was a professional bad-writing doctor. He also taught night classes in composition. He was fond of writing *WDW* in large red letters next to a bad sentence. The student was then required to rephrase it in *who does what* form. Later, I tried the technique. Here is an example of *WDW-ing* one student:

Original: Accordingly, there is a tremendous emphasis on PE and recreation beginning in the junior high which accounts for the significant increase in the accident rate for grades 7-12.

First Rewrite: Accordingly, the schools emphasize PE and recreation beginning in the junior high which accounts for the significant increase in the accident rate for grades 7-12. (I said: "Try *WDW* some more.")

Second Rewrite: Beginning in junior high, the schools emphasize PE and recreation. This emphasis causes the significant increase.... (I said: "Look again; try the real *WDW;* what is *causing* something to happen?")

Third Rewrite: Beginning in junior high, schools emphasize PE and recreation for the first time. For example, about forty percent more students play touch football, softball, and soccer. So, starting in grade 7, the accident rate in school increases.

The result of *WDW-ing* sentences is wide and deep—curiously so. In its emphasis on "looking again," I am reminded of Louis Agassiz (1807-1873), Nathaniel Shaler, and the fish. Professor Agassiz gave student Shaler a small fish and told him to study it, which he did for a week. Agassiz ignored him throughout the week, so Shaler went on to study for another "hundred hours or so," at which time he informed the master that he knew all about that fish. Agassiz disagreed, and Shaler continued fishing. In "another week of ten hours a day labor" on the same fish—now decrepit—Shaler had results that satisfied his professor.[17]

Who does what-ing is partly a set of implied commands relating semantics, syntax, and the situation. The student is told: look at the situation, find the action(s) involved, and put them into an SVO pattern. Keep doing this—keep looking at the fish—until you learn enough to straighten out your sentences. If you need more sentences, use them. *WDW* obviously emphasizes predication; and, in trying to make his predication clearer, the writer will often automatically throw some material into an opener. As he gains readability in successive revisions, the writer employs the predicative and sentence-unit strategies. In the example given, the student also used coordination *(touch football, softball, and soccer)*. Specificity is one of the benefits of *WDW.* Another is getting rid of bad passives, which tend to disappear when the rule is applied.

The *who does what* technique bothers my grammatical friends. They say it is too limited as technique and too weak theoretically. Actually, it is often not limited at all. I have seen students range through logic, grammar, syntax, idiom, semantics, and several well-nibbled pastures of their major field before finishing a single *WDW-ified* sentence. It is true that they weren't aware of what they were doing grammatically, but they did know they were trying to harmonize or fit their perceptions about a situation with sentences that described it. This is a considerable advance.

It should be mentioned that in trying for a *WDW* pattern, students may get an SV or SV₁ C pattern. This does not worry them. They don't know the difference, and I can't take the time to teach them formal grammar. It doesn't worry me either.

THE RULE OF NEARNESS

"Put things that belong together *near* each other—as close as possible."

Bad Sentence:	The cost of work which had been accomplished in the Assembly Section before the last inspection date could be difficult to determine due to faulty records.

The first thing you might notice about that sentence is the wide separation of subject and verb, a violation of the rule of nearness. One tactic is to ask the writer to apply *who does what,* and keep on applying it until the situation is clear and the nearness problem is solved.

Revised Sentence:	Since your Assembly Section lost its records for June, I can't determine the cost of work done before the last inspection date.

Here are textbook examples of violations of the nearness rule:

1. The miniskirt is *in the eyes of the fashion industry* a dead issue.
2. How many minority group members are *by actual count of the Census Bureau or its state counterparts* on welfare?

3. Gambetta's indifference destroyed, *if we can believe Denis Brogan*, what hope there was of a reconciliation.
4. The nations of the Third World have, *in the fifteen years since the Bandung Conference*, looked in vain for a leader and a program.[18]

Such sentences can be repaired using techniques mentioned earlier.

One minor application of the rule of nearness involves the split infinitive, which violates it. I could care less about any usage rule on split infinitives, just as I couldn't care less about usage rules on the first four words of this sentence. But it is true that *to* customarily belongs next to the verb it's a sign of. Try counting the infinitives in a decently edited magazine, and see how few—if any—are split. This is a useful activity in airport waiting rooms. If you are seen doing it with magazines like *Playboy*, other passengers will respect you and keep a safe distance.

Once, while counting infinitives in an airport, I found one magazine's drama critic declaring that "the play shows you a senile and bitter Salieri, reliving the events which brought him to ultimately accuse himself of having murdered Mozart." One suspects the writer meant *ultimately* to modify *brought*.

READABILITY FORMULAS

The most popular—and probably the best of the formulas—is the *fog index* employed by the Gunning-Mueller Clear Writing Institute. Here is how you compute the index:

1. Find the average number of words per sentence in a sample of your writing one hundred to two hundred words long. Treat clearly independent clauses as separate sentences. Example: "In school we read; we learned; we improved." This counts as three sentences.
2. Calculate the percentage of words having three or more syllables. Don't count capitalized words, easy combinations like "pawnbroker," or verbs that reach three syllables by addition of -es or -ed.
3. Add the average sentence length to the percentage of big words and multiply the total by 0.4. The resulting number

is the years of schooling needed to understand what you've written. If the piece of writing you are analyzing is lengthy, take other samples at random, repeat the process and average the results.

Academicians tend to be scornful of such formulas. I don't care much for them myself, and not just because they quantify without reference to meaning. They also tell us nothing about the grammatical operations that lie behind readable (or unreadable) sentences. The only thing they have in their favor is that for some writers they work very well. I've seen startling results with engineers and businessmen after application of the Gunning-Mueller formula described above. *The Wall Street Journal* reports:

> . . . the rules of clear writing are news to many corporate authors and they can benefit dramatically. John Lane, superintendent of technical information at Ethyl Corp.'s Michigan Research Center, says Gunning seminars brought "absolutely amazing" improvement in company research reports. In one test, 11 chemists who wrote at an average fog index of 18 dropped to below 13. Mr. Lane has since developed his own in-house program and now offers training to customer companies as well.[19]

I have used readability formulas with college students, but not with much success. It is true that they write better after a few sessions with a formula; but the effect does not last. More important, they never learn *why* their writing was unreadable in the first place.

One problem with the formulas is that we don't know what they measure, or whether different formulas measure the same thing. This report from the Document Design Center gives an idea of the difficulty:

> The Food and Drug Administration (FDA) measured the "readability" of a number of prototype drug information brochures ("patient package inserts"), using several "readability formulas" that establish a grade level for a text. The results were that different formulas produced very different grade levels for the same material, differing by as many as 9.7 grade levels. Not much internal validity there.[20]

TEACHING READABILITY—A FEW CONCLUSIONS

Every writer creates sentences from a large mix of variables. Included are variables like stance, nature and development of arguments, the strategies and requirements of organization. The successful writer balances a number of demands made upon him before he even starts to put words down. And then there's the fact that the language is not a bit docile. Richard Weaver remarked that "language is not a purely passive instrument":

> ... while you are doing something with it, it is doing something with you, or with your intention. It does not exactly fight back; rather it has a set of postures and balances which somehow modify your thrusts and holds. The sentence form is certainly one of these. You pour into it your meaning, and it deflects, and molds into certain shapes.[21]

Students need to learn that even the most experienced writer is forced to wrestle with a sentence, to make it take alternative shapes and supply different messages. A dozen years ago, a student of mine wrote a sentence that I wanted to improve but could not: *One of the most striking features of plays in this genre [modern realistic drama] is the compromise between the events of everyday life and traditional forms of art.*

When I tried a revision of the sentence, I wrote this: *In modern realistic drama, the most striking feature is that the author is forced to compromise between the demands of traditional art and the events, as he experiences them, of everyday life.* The revision was no better than the original; I didn't know the subject and was afraid to say anything specific about it.

So I wrote a note to my colleague, Charles Shattuck, an expert in drama and one of the best academic writers I know. I asked him: "What do I do with this sentence to make it more readable?" Here is his answer:

> First, I would change *the most striking* because *the most* here is simply not true. I would also change *author* to *playwright*— for exactness. But let me try some other versions of the sentence:
> (A) *One of the most striking features of modern realistic*

*drama is the compromise which playwrights always make be-
tween the demands of traditional art and the events of everyday
life.*

But this sentence is still a joylessly long buzz of words. I'll
try again:

(B) *One very striking feature of modern realistic drama is its
compromise between reality and art. However earnestly the playwright wants to depict everyday life, he alters it to fit it into
dramatic form.*

Once more:

(C) *The trouble with modern realistic drama is that form
compromises fact. (Plus second sentence to explain.)*

You will object that in my second and third tries I've spoiled
the game by using more than one sentence. This, however, is the
best way out of the difficulty—the real difficulty being that the
original "bad" sentence attempts to include too much. So, to put
it effectively, one expresses the nugget idea in a sentence of
the fewest possible words; then, in a sentence or two following,
one expands and explains. The opening sentence may be simply
factual, or enigmatic, or even sensational: its communicative
intent is to catch attention, even perhaps to startle and
challenge attention, so that the reader wants to read on.

I'll try a razzle-dazzle version:

(D) *Realistic drama is a lie. The playwright pretends to show
the truth of everyday life, to tell it like it is. But he is so trapped
by the demands of dramatic technique that he compromises the
truth, or even forgets it, long before his play is written.*

Maybe I'd better not try any more! Thanks for the game:
Better than solitaire, which I never play anyway.

As he wrestled with the sentence, Professor Shattuck employed
several techniques of gaining readability. Perhaps more discussions like his should be put in textbooks—teacherly *protocols*, as it
were—to illustrate how to come to terms with idea and structure.
Such discussions might tell us more than we presently know about
teaching readability, and also show us how to create the "single

perception" which must be shared by teacher and student—editor and writer—in order for improvement in writing to occur.

It is true that the good writer often doesn't use the neat rules for readability I have laid out in this essay. Sometimes it appears that the better he is, the less he uses them. But the problem in modern writing is not that of the writer who usually succeeds whatever he does, but that of the many writers who are not succeeding consistently no matter what they do. They need help; and if rules for readability can give a little help, it would be unwise to ignore them.

2 Nobody Are Perfect: On Shaping a Course in Grammar*

". . . I know grammar by ear only, not by rote, not by the rules. A generation ago I knew the rules—knew them by heart, word for word, though not their meanings—and I still know one of them: the one which says—which says—but never mind, it will come back to me presently."
Mark Twain, *Autobiography*[1]

Anyone who teaches grammar has to make a decision about needs. What do his students need? What does society need? Or, to restate the question, how much grammatical knowledge does society expect from students who have finished a unit of education—junior high, high school, college? Finally, what does the discipline of grammar (an old and honorable area of study) need from those who teach and learn it? One cannot ignore the requirements of student, society, discipline. Each has its problems and demands. In response to each, a teacher should tell the truth—but whose truth?

---

*This essay should be read with Chapter 1, "Teaching the Readable Sentence." I wish to thank my students in the years 1964-1980—about 1300 of them—who taught me much of what I think I know about grammar and its relation to writing.

Such questions are not easy to answer, as the following tales will illustrate.

I

Last year my wife Charlene and I wrote a letter on jargon and gobbledygook to *The Wall Street Journal.* In it, we used the expression *none are.* After the publication of our letter, the grammatical roof fell in.

Apparently, *The Wall Street Journal* is read everywhere and by everybody. We got letters from Australia, Japan, Canada; from California, Mississippi, Michigan, New York, Florida; and from points in between. We heard from bankers, lawyers, journalists, businessmen, school teachers, college professors. All of them agreed with the point of our letter; but almost to a man—and definitely to a woman—they were unhappy, caustic, even downright indignant about our use of the expression *none are.* We got two anonymous letters. And there was an anonymous postcard, with these words neatly printed on it: NOBODY ARE PERFECT.

O brave new world, that has such grammarpersons in it!

Ours was the fate of teachers who are injudicious enough to make judgments on language while using standard idiom. It seems that many educated Americans react almost allergically to certain normal patterns of speech and writing. Hoping to mollify the readers of the *Journal,* we published a second letter in that newspaper, pointing out that *none are* has been accepted by modern chams on usage from Fowler to Follett. We thought that quoting an authority like H. W. Fowler would reduce the rage of some of our correspondents, particularly those who taught English.

This didn't work. Our readers were still angry. One English teacher (high school) wrote us that she did not believe the authorities were right on the issue—she would continue to teach the singularity of *none.* Besides, she asked, who was H. W. Fowler?

Perhaps we should have quoted Professor Thomas Pyles on *none are:*

The usage in question is first recorded in the ninth century in the writings of Alfred the Great. More recent occurrences cited by the *OED*, which points out that the plural usage is "now the commoner . . . the sing [ular] being expressed by *no one*," are from the writings of . . . Dryden, Goldsmith, Burke, and Southey; and Otto Jespersen adds occurrences from St. Thomas More, Shakespeare, Dr. Johnson ("None are wretched but by their own fault"), Scott, Charlotte Brontë, Ruskin, Morris, Shaw, Stevenson, and Kipling.[2]

Or we could have cited Lindley Murray (1745-1826), no grammatical radical he:

> *None* is used in both numbers: as, *"None* is so deaf as he that will not hear;" *"None* of those are equal to these." It seems originally to have signified, according to its derivation, *not one*, and therefore to have had no plural; but there is good authority for the use of it in the plural number: as, *"None* that *go* unto her *return* again." *Prov.* ii. 19. "Terms of peace *were none* vouchsaf'd." Milton.[3]

Well, it would take more than Milton to justify grammar's ways to some men—or to explain why grammar is for many Americans a hobby to be taken with violent seriousness, like wine-making or continuous (continual?) amorous adventuring. At the same time, most Americans think of grammar and the grammarian as they think of medicine and the physician. He who has studied the subject and has the appropriate letters after his name should be able to operate on the patient, provide medication, stop the pain, *do something.*

There's the rub. More or less, we all have the same language and are afflicted by the same linguistic diseases. But for several reasons, the cures don't work with most people—the grammatical information they swallow might as well be mixed in a hollow skull by a stone-age medicine man. Many of the readers of *The Wall Street Journal* will never accept *none are* as correct, no matter how many authorities the Tibbettses cite. They will think that we are putting them on in some elaborate way: that for reasons of our own, we created an elaborate professorial hoax, rather as a cynical economist might prove through complicated argument that "inflation" does not really exist.

To readers of the *Journal*, both money and grammar are entities. A dollar bill and a verb are not just names, but discrete things you use every day. *Dollar* and *verb* should act as constants in ordinary financial and linguistic transactions. If you explain that *dollar*, as a financial term, may be more stable hour by hour from Maine to California than *verb*, as a linguistic term, you may be accused of mere cleverness. Instability in the important aspects of one's life cannot be tolerated. The matter should be debated calmly, concretely, and in specific simplicities.

Let the Grammarian and the Educated Person meet in a neutral corner and agree, for example, that *run* can be a verb: *I run.* But then the Grammarian points out that other forms of the word are not necessarily verbs. *Running* can be noun or adjective, a "verbal." He supplies explanations. The Educated Person accepts them, but ground he thought was firm is beginning to tremble beneath his feet. He grows suspicious and reaches for a weapon, a grammatical shibboleth:

Educated Person:	Why does *nobody* take the singular and *none* take the singular or plural?
Grammarian:	From a historical standpoint, the answer is not necessarily a simple one. But we can begin by saying that usage decides such issues and that . . . .
Educated Person:	But who decides usage?
Grammarian:	Why, you do—you and the other educated users of the language.
Educated Person:	It is gratifying to have such power, and now I know I have it, I hereby promulgate this law: *"None has been and always shall remain—SINGULAR (no matter what those in outer darkness may claim).* Now let us hear the National Anthem.

Professor Francis Weeks is Professor of English, Executive Director of the American Business Communication Association, and an internationally known expert on business writing. He is also an active consultant to businesses. Businessmen often say to him: "We know that our grammar in memos, letters, and reports is bad. Please correct it. Help us to never make those horrible mistakes again which ruin our writing."

Professor Weeks is an honest man. He looks at their writing samples and says: "You make hardly any mistakes in grammar. So few indeed that to discuss your grammatical errors would be to waste your company's money." Businessmen do not like this answer. Would a time-and-motion consultant have the gall to stand before them and state that the company could improve neither its use of hours nor its elegance of movements?

Professor Weeks then tells them: "Your grammar is not at fault, and you don't need what you call *grammar*. Rather you have other problems—weak interest in the reader, faulty thought, carelessness, disorganization, jargon, general unreadability." These are not the bones businessmen want to chew on, but at least for a while they are distracted from that old devil, grammar.

I have a friend, about fifty, who used to be a professor of classics in a private university. A new administration decided to cut costs and therefore cut the Classics Department. My friend went by stages to several places of employment, including a factory that made mattresses. He is now teaching English in a rural Illinois high school. I asked him what he taught. "Mainly," he said, "I teach grammar—parts of speech, phrases, clauses, all the hard words like *participle* and *gerund*. The parents in my farming community don't care what 'English' you teach so long as you teach grammar. And you'd better make it incomprehensible, or they will think you're not doing the job."

My friend's community was devoutly Protestant—but those farmers had got themselves a priest of sorts in the public high school. I checked on him the other day and he is still there, showering on his flock grammatical blessings and *vade mecums*, which even in our hugely fertile corn country usually fall among thorns.

II

So—we have at least two broad issues in the general problem: Whose needs shall we satisfy? Whose truths shall we teach? The rest of this essay is an account of one resolution of these issues.

One week after I started teaching at the University of Illinois, the department head called me to his office. He said, "Professor X has been promoted to an administrative job and so will not be doing the grammar course for teachers. I'd like you to take it over." That was the only time I ever tried to refuse a course assignment. I had taught grammar in three other universities and had failed at it. I could see little connection between learning it and learning to write. I was convinced that for students the best way to learn "grammar" was to learn a foreign language well. The head reminded me gently that I was an untenured newcomer to the department. I started teaching the grammar course the next day.

This is my sixteenth year of teaching *English 302, Grammar and Usage*. The number designation means that it is an advanced course for juniors, seniors, and graduate students. In the middle sixties we had hundreds of English Education majors and minors, and they all had to take English 302, of which six sections were taught each semester.

At first, I just staggered through the course, teaching from standard traditional textbooks. A couple of years later, I rebuilt it and added elements of the "new" grammars, along with usage material based on historical studies. For usage, the debates over Webster's *Third* provided a contemporary context.[4] In a few years, I was requiring numerous outside readings in the library, assigning several short papers, and using five textbooks in class. By 1970, English 302 involved a wide range of information about language and its history. It was what we professors like to call a "solid advanced course."

At that time English 302 was a grammar course responding (I thought) to the needs of the discipline and of young people about to enter the teaching profession. They were learning about grammars and writing the standard short term papers about them. Our discussions were theoretical and elevated—after all, it was an advanced course. But one thing troubled me. By a sort of accident, when I had twenty minutes of empty space toward the end of the term, I gave a diagnostic test to my students. It was a standard high school objective test on errors in grammar and usage. But I changed the test so that each question also had to be explained and discussed.

My students could not do that test. A few days later, I gave them another one, also specially made for the occasion. They performed no better. I took a number of important items from the major usage manuals, made up a short test, and gave it to them. Same result. I gave them a dozen snippets of bad writing from newspapers, magazines, and term papers. I wrote a trick question for the snippets, asking students to identify six bad passages and to explain why they were bad. I also told them there was a trick in the question. In addition, I asked: "How do the six good snippets use proper grammar and usage?" My students—all of whom were going to be teachers of English—proved to be no better informed than readers of *The Wall Street Journal*. They could not tell good from bad, or defend their opinions. Clearly I was doing something wrong.

My mistake was one that no teacher should make. I had paid too little attention to the students and what they knew. I was not "starting where they were." Furthermore, I was playing too seriously the role of professor in a university that valued theoretical scholarship above everything. The most damning phrase that could be applied to an advanced course taken by juniors, seniors, and graduate students was "nuts and bolts." An advanced course had to have advanced textbooks, advanced reading lists, and an advanced point of view. This meant I should assume that students already knew the sort of grammar found in elementary textbooks, and that I was obligated to teach them something else—almost anything else—so long as it wasn't nuts and bolts. I was fulfilling every need in sight except theirs.

As the years went by, I paid more attention to the students. Of course our student body was changing, particularly that part of it which took English 302. The number of students in English Education plummeted. The other professors managed to get out of teaching the course by promotion, retirement, or death. By the middle 1970s, I was the only one teaching it. But I had more students than ever. They came from all over the campus. In one section, the enrollment information on undergraduate majors showed pre-law, nonacademic (a secretary), political science, finance, creative writing, psychology, business administration, sociology, English, social work, accounting, speech education, chemical engineering, history, vo tech, journalism, biology, electrical engineering, and philosophy. Five other students in the section were in the English-teaching program. One nonacademic person was a computer specialist. The graduate students came from law, secondary education, family consumption economics, agricultural economics, accounting, and agronomy.

When asked why they took the course, here is a sample of what the students wrote:

> I want to be an editor, and thought this course would help me.
> Grammar is good for an engineering student to know.
> Have to take the course (I'm in teacher ed.—English).
> Don't know any grammer [sic].
> Accountants have to write more than anybody knows.
> Want to pass the LSAT.
> I'm a law student and having trouble with my writing.
> Want to go to grad school [from a biology major].
> I'm writing a computer program for high school students [from a full-time professional in Special Programs].
> Thought it would help me understand my own writing better [from a major in Creative Writing].
> I have to write my boss's letters [from a secretary].

A theme is represented in these comments, one that has been a constant in the course for almost a decade. It might be expressed: *For various reasons, I want to understand and control my language better. Can you help me do this?*

There was a considerable challenge here. In one typical class, thirty-two of thirty-seven students were taking English 302 as an elective. Five would-be English teachers were taking it because they were required to. I had to create a course that would satisfy all of them—one that would be reasonably responsive to the standards of the discipline and to the requirements of whichever "real world" they chose to enter.

In rebuilding the course, I dropped the theoretical textbooks in favor of a standard handbook in grammar. The library reading list disappeared in favor of short mimeographed passages ranging from Shakespeare to E. B. White to Hemingway. The course is now taught mainly from mimeographed material (good and bad writing samples), with the handbook as a reference. I believe that in a course like this, all students should get roughly the same information and training, whether they are going to be teachers, businessmen, or scientists, whether they are sophomores or second-year graduate students. After all, they have the same language and the same problems with it. Teaching, writing, and thinking about the language—all should be brought closer together.

Such were the needs I tried to make decisions about. They were made, of course, in a context that tended to control decision-making. One important controlling element was and is the course itself. Students may come and go, but it seems that English 302 will endure forever. Where is it going now?

Here is a rough outline of the present course:

Definitions of *grammar, rhetoric, usage, idiom*
Parts of speech
Sentence skeletons (SV, SVO, SVC, etc.)
Readability: sentence units and predication, as detailed
in Chapter 1
Clauses
Verbs vs. verbals
Phrases
Parallelism (coordination) as detailed in Chapter 1
Levels of generality—how gained by use of grammar and words
The basic grammatical operations: predication, modification,
coordination, subordination, complementation, explanation
(includes absolutes and certain so-called adverbials)
Usage:
Principles: accuracy and appropriateness
Question and problems concerning metaphor, denotation, con-
notation, abstraction, etc.
Mixed diction
Usage books: Fowler, Evans, Bernstein, Gowers, Morris and
Morris
Grammatical errors: from faulty agreement to the sentence
fragment
Editing: problems and solutions
Punctuation
A gathering of styles: from Shakespeare to Mailer

III

Such a course outline provides bones but not, necessarily, nourish-ment for the hungry. We all know that when students study grammar, they ordinarily don't learn much. They memorize rules and forms, but do not generally perceive them as being part of their mental equipment or linguistic technique. They understand grammar best when it combines activities involving terms, patterns, devices, signals—and practice. Any time you speak or write, you are a grammarian. The problem is to speak and write—to be the normal human grammarian—while watching yourself do it. To perceive while practicing, to practice while perceiving. As given to students, my basic premise is: the language is a *code* and *coding system;* you are at once a coding system and a decoder. Learn and apply the major strategies of the code. Then you will both understand and control your language better. But never perfectly. For the code and system are imperfect, full of flaws and unexpected quirks and short circuits.

In the fifteen weeks of English 302, I emphasize the major elements of the code and shamelessly cut grammatical corners. For example, I tell students: "Use *who*. Don't bother about *whom;* it's not worth the trouble, except perhaps with prepositions: for *whom*, by *whom.*" I am one of those mentioned by Sir Ernest Gowers in *Plain Words*, who believes that *whom* is "a mischief-maker":

> The proper use of the two words should present no difficulty. But we are so unaccustomed to different case-formations in English that when we are confronted with them we are liable to lose our heads. In the matter of *who* and *whom* good writers have for centuries been perverse in refusing to do what the grammarians tell them. They will insist on writing sentences like "Who should I see there?" (Addison), "Ferdinand whom they suppose is drowned" (Shakespeare), "Whom say men that I am?" (translators of the Bible). Now any schoolboy can see that, by the rules, *who* in the first quotation, being the object of *see*, ought to be *whom*, and that *whom* in the second and third quotations, being in the one the subject of *is*, and in the other the complement of *am*, ought to be *who*. What then is the ordinary man to believe? There are some who would have us do away with *whom* altogether, as nothing but a mischief-maker. That might be a useful way out. But then, as was asked in the correspondence columns of the *Spectator* by one who signed himself "A. Woodowl" (31st December, 1948):
>
> > Regarding the suggested disuse of *whom*, may I ask by who a lead can be given? To who, to wit, of the "cultured" authorities can we appeal to boo *whom* and to boom *who?*[5]

A student asked me: "Why do you ignore *interjections* and *articles?*" Because the native speaker who is, as you are, a college junior and an engineer does not need to know about them. Go study them if you wish. The information can't hurt you. "Why," asks another, "did you say nothing about the classification of pronouns in the textbook—*personal, relative, reflexive, intensive, interrogative, demonstrative, reciprocal, indefinite?*" Because that classification—at least in your case—unlocks no mysteries, teaches no skill. Again: if you want to know more about pronouns, be my guest. Or, rather, the library's. The complete grammars will explain all.

My goal of instruction is to teach the grammatical names and operations that students need to know as writers and critics of writing. They should know the names and functions of parts of speech, phrases, clauses, full sentences. They need practical work on usage, diction, meaning. It is often more useful to discuss a word as a chunk of meaning than as a part of speech, although both descriptions may come into play at times.

Grammatical information is most applicable when terms, operations, and choices are clear to students. For instance, the grammar of phrases means little to them no matter how it is approached. One reason may be that the terminology is clumsy and opaque. *Participial*, as a term, might as well be Greek. Perhaps another—more fundamental—reason is that for the native speaker phrases tend to be invisible, more so than other parts of the code. Consider:

She *might have done* that.
Don and Jerry are here.
It's *in the attic.*

The code works so smoothly in handling the choices involved in each of these sentences, that the native speaker does not think of them *as* choices, even when studying the phrasal system. I notice that students do not talk about phrases as they do clauses, parts of speech, or dubious usages. Unless a phrase is set off by punctuation, or is awkward or illogical, it is invisible to them. Even when it is punctuated, they may prefer to consider a phrase as a rhetorical unit of some kind, rather than as a grammatical construction.

Some of the problems of teaching grammar arise from certain accepted ideas about grammatical information. Textbooks—and teachers as well—have often pretended that this information is pretty much cut and dried. For instance:

Subordinate Ideas

When ideas in a sentence are unequal in rank, the ideas of lower rank are subordinate. (*Sub-* means "under" or "lower.") If the idea of lower rank is expressed in a clause, the clause is a *subordinate* clause. The main idea of the sentence is expressed in an *independent* clause.

Examples:

The pilot, who was a veteran flyer, brought her crippled plane down safely. [Independent clause—greater emphasis: *The pilot brought her crippled plane down safely;* subordinate clause—lesser emphasis: *who was a veteran flyer.*]

Because each of them was politically ambitious, the council members rarely supported one another's proposals. [Main clause—greater emphasis: *the council members rarely supported one another's proposals;* subordinate clause—lesser emphasis: *Because each of them was politically ambitious.*][6]

Thus Warriner's *English Grammar and Composition,* one of the most widely used high school writing texts in America. In order to make this information teachable (and teacher-proof), Warriner gives the student partly false information. Subordinate clauses don't necessarily contain ideas "of lower rank," as the examples given illustrate. In the first, *who was a veteran flyer* in many full contexts would be more important than the idea in the main clause. It is possible to say the same about the subordinate clause in the second example. Why the bad information? Because the textbook author and the teacher must both pretend that grammar can be easily learned. Surely, they say to the student, you can learn anything so clearly defined and *regularized* as the subordinate clause, which is always tucked safely into its little bed of lesser emphasis.

Such regularizing information is ultimately confusing enough that students don't retain it. Or, if they do, they don't benefit from it. Clauses are regularized into the classification of *noun, adjective,* and *adverb.* This works only with the first two classes. To students, adverbial clauses don't look adverbial because, one suspects, many of them aren't. They are "explainers" rather than modifiers. For many years I have been advising students when we classify clauses to avoid looking for adverb clauses as such. "See if the clause is noun or adjective; if it isn't, throw it into the adverb class and forget about it."

The subordinate clause is recognizable and clear in the grammatical code for reasons other than those ordinarily emphasized in high school textbooks. It has a subordinating signal acting like a vivid, flashing light in the sentence: *who, that, which, how, when, in order that,* etc. (The part of speech of this signal is, for the writer, relatively unimportant.) The clause also has *predication:* the subject-verb relation (see Chapter 1). Without these two characteristics, a reader would not be able to distinguish the subordinate clause from other competing elements in the code.

In order for grammatical instruction to be efficient for the writer, it should fit the coding system reasonably well. The code says, for example, that subjects and verbs agree. But it does not—cannot—say that they always agree or that the idea of agreement can be defined precisely. Thus *cats meow,* a *dog barks, people sing,* but *none is* or *are.* A student wants to know the parts of speech in this awkward but grammatical sentence: *Some people ask such a question before doing the job that they are always told to do.*

Answer: consult the *code table* for parts of speech—

Nouns:	
	} *name*
Pronouns:	
Verbs:	} *state*
Adverbs:	
	} *modify*
Adjectives:	
Conjunctions:	
	} *join*
Prepositions:	

The student and I talk about the sentence:

Nouns are *people, question, job.* Modifying words are *some* and *always.* For *some,* use the slot system: _____ noun. Analogy: *Dirty people* is similar to *some people; some* is an adjective.

Objection: why couldn't *some* be a pronoun—*some* standing for *people*, as in *Some are going to run?* No, I say, you are changing the construction; it's not *some ask*, but *some people ask*.

Verbs are *ask* and *are*. The student wonders, why not the whole thing, *are told to do?* Yes, call the whole thing the verb; consider the verb as a chunk made up of smaller chunks. Another question: what is *doing?* I say: how are *before doing* and *after the game* alike? Answer: they both follow the preposition-noun pattern. (Think of this mnemonic pattern from football: *hut-one, hut-two, prep-noun*. Silly mnemonics often work better than sensible ones.)

What is *that?* the student asks. Answer: ignore it for the time being; we will take it up later, under *clauses*.

More discussion, until *such* is left. I say that I don't know about *such*. I tell the class: bring me some *such* phrases tomorrow; each *such* you bring in should act as a different part of speech.

In the next meeting of the class, students say they have found these *suches:*

Adjective: *such* people
Pronoun: consider it as *such*
Adverb: *such* happy days
Pronoun: *such* were the consequences
   ?   on *such* a day as this

I suggest: consider *such a* as an adjectival idiom modifying *day*.

Students remind me that we put off discussing *that* in the sample sentence. Let's keep putting it off, I say.

Putting a subject off implies an efficacious ordering of instructional materials. Students appear to learn more efficiently when specific pieces of grammatical information are presented in a certain order. "Logical" order is not necessarily the best. They must learn the levels of grammatical analysis:

Level Five: Running prose (e.g., sentences in a paragraph)
Level Four: The sentence (base and free units, etc.)
Level Three: The clause
Level Two: The phrase
Level One: The part of speech

Knowing and understanding these levels is mandatory for intelligent discussion of grammatical issues. Yet I have found that the

standard logical technique of moving from the small to the large—
here, from the lower to the higher level—works against efficient
learning at two points.

First, for the reasons already mentioned, students have difficulty with Level Two, phrases. Phrases do not sufficiently stand out
in the hierarchy of analysis. Second, a study of Level Four,
including base and free units (see Chapter 1) is inefficient if it is
done later than the clause (Level Three): students keep confusing
unit with *clause* and *phrase*. They will be quite confused by sentence
bases, which by nature can contain more than one clause.

My solution has been to study Level One first; jump to Level
Four for the material on predication and sentence units (as
discussed in Chapter 1); then move down to the clause, which is a
fairly rigid and predictable structure. The phrase I treat as a
grammatical unit "larger" than the part of speech but "smaller"
than the clause—*smaller* in that it lacks predication.

I have tried teaching the five levels in various orders. The order
of One, Four, Three, Two, Five seems to work best, with the fewest
putting-off delays and the best general comprehension of grammatical analysis and rhetorical technique. Even so, some putting-
off is necessary here and there. On the parts-of-speech level, I
decline comment on words used as subordinating signs because to
get into clauses at that stage hurts more than helps.

On the other hand, a discussion of *sentence skeletons* (SV, SVO,
SVC, etc.) is helpful almost from the beginning. A student benefits
from discussing skeletons in every part of the course, since they help
explain a number of things, from the empty *it* or *there* in the
expletive to the way meanings are transmitted by clause types.

Before covering Level Five, the class spends about three weeks
on diction and usage. Much of the last part of the course is spent on
three rough sections in Level Five: readability, editing bad sentences, and sentence rhetoric—the effective shaping of sentences in
a paragraph context.

IV

Years ago, when our English Department taught six sections of
English 302, most of us teachers used Nick Hook's *Modern American Grammar and Usage.* Using Hook's text made teaching the
usage portion of the course quite easy. Each chapter of the text

covered usage problems appropriate to the topic being taught. When his text went out of print, I had some difficulty finding materials that were both teachable and relevant.

Too many usage questions are related to a teacher's quirks and special interests, or to technical matters that most students will not pursue no matter how you encourage (or threaten) them. I gave up assigning short readings in Fowler, Evans, Bernstein, etc., although I still require that every student dip into the major works on usage.

Sir Ernest Gowers quotes G. M. Young: "The final cause of speech is to get an idea as exactly as possible out of one mind into another. Its formal cause therefore is such choice and disposition of words as will achieve this end most economically."[7]

Following Young at a respectful distance, I treat *usage* as a question of how one chooses the most accurate, precise, and appropriate words and constructions in each circumstance. Practically speaking, students and I are interested in how writers and editors make their decisions—how they retain flexibility in word choice while making sense.

Students have been misinformed regarding usage. For one thing, they have been taught to believe that usages are generally either right or wrong. This has comical consequences. A middle-aged candidate for the Ph.D. in music asked me last week, "Can you use *however* as the first word in a sentence?" Sure, I said. "Well," he said, "you can't do it in the Music Department. It's an unwritten law." As we talked more about this and other usages, I was once again made aware of the American compulsion to discuss usages disjunctively. Is it proper to say thus-and-such? *Answer yes or no.* If you answer *maybe* or *sometimes* or (worse yet) try to rephrase the question, there goes your credibility. Before dropping English 302 about mid-term, a law student told me, "I took this course to get answers, and all you give me is questions."

For another thing, students have been led to believe in the myth of formal usage. This troublesome doctrine, this misplaced faith in the formal, irritates me so much that early in the course I deal in exaggeration and tirade:

Do not speak to me of formal English but of good English and bad; that which communicates and that which doesn't; that which does not offend and that which does; that which is believable and that which isn't. Formal English is what is wrong with our lovely language; formal English is the gobbledygook and jargon of lawyers, federal officials, university deans, and many of your lousy textbooks. It is cant and professorese like *concept, parenting,* and *structure* (as a verb). It is likely that you require formal English only three times in your life: when you are christened, when you are married, and when you are dead and being prayed over. If you are elected President of this Republic, you are allowed to use formal English in your inaugural address. Otherwise, stay away from it; it is the curse of the thinking writer. *Write as you speak, when you're speaking very well.*

To emphasize the importance of flexibility in questions of usage, I insist that students try to give more than one answer to a question. Thus the avoidance technique, explained in a handout:

An *avoidance* is not a "cop-out," but a valid way around a grammatical problem. Instead of confronting the problem and attempting to solve it with a standard solution, you avoid it by using a different construction. In this way, you may not be locked into a fixed response to a problem. Your writing can take on a new flexibility if you recognize that you have choices other than the standard solutions. As an example, consider the familiar problem of agreement with *either-or* and *neither-nor.* It is not hard to remember that with singular nouns in the subject, these pairs take singular verbs. You simply memorize this fact and apply it when necessary:
Neither the car *nor* the truck *was* stolen.
But what do you use when there is one car and two trucks?
Neither the car *nor* the trucks *was* (?) *were* (?) stolen.
Neither *was* nor *were* sounds right, although the grammatical rule says that *were* is the proper choice—"the verb should agree with the nearer of its subjects."
It is often possible to *avoid* such a problem (and the possibility of error) by using one of several different constructions that will say pretty much the same thing. Here are a few:
Problem:
Neither the car nor the trucks *was* (?) *were* (?) stolen.
Avoidances:

The car *was* not stolen. Neither *were* the trucks.
The trucks *were* not stolen. Nor *was* the car.
The trucks and the car *were* not stolen.
The car and the trucks *were* still there.
The car *was* not stolen, and the trucks *weren't* either.
The trucks and the car *have not been* stolen.
The thieves *left* the car and the trucks.[8]

To dramatize the importance of word choice, the students and I do critical exercises involving words in a sentence context.

Sentence: Sam's statement was clear; he inferred that this type of angry, bottle-throwing fan is really belittling the coach.

Criticism: The sentence is okay to the semicolon. Then it falls apart. If Sam made the statement, he should be *implying* not *inferring.* But if his statement is *clear,* it is probably not an implication. *Type?* How can there be more than one type of *angry bottle-throwing fan?* The most inappropriate word in the sentence is *belittle,* a mild term that does not fit the action; any fan who throws bottles is intending mayhem, perhaps murder—hardly belittlement.

Sentence: The loss of credibility represents a necessary foundation upon which authority structures are undermined.

Criticism: The words are too abstract, vague, general. The skeleton is SVO: *loss represents foundation.* This is a bad metaphor: the absence of something cannot be or represent a foundation. The words tell us that *authority structures* are undermined on top of a *foundation,* which is impossible.

Why does the typical undergraduate have so much trouble with words? Of course, they are slippery beasts at best. One reason is that inexperienced writers have had little practice in banging words around; they need batting practice:

Generalized outline	(Isn't an outline *generalized* by definition?)
Loud, erratic rhythm	(A rhythm isn't a noise; therefore it can't be *loud.)*
Center around	(No, *center on,* and *cluster around.)*
Highlights of my religion	(What do you mean by *highlights?* your religious *beliefs, theories, tenets, doctrines, principles, dogmas?)*
Very unknown	(Can you really be *unknowner* than *unknown?)*
All inclusive	(Impossible; *inclusive* includes *all.)*

One can, if one wishes, hear arguments in favor of such expressions. If you can have a loud tie, why not a loud rhythm? For the point is not to limit expression or to defang the language so that it can only glumly gum its ideas, but to encourage students to use the language clearly, accurately, economically. *And to think about words and the choice of them.*

To encourage such thinking, we spend a day or two on metaphor and the traps therein. I point out that misuse of metaphor is increasing; it is one of the symptoms of the "writing crisis." A reporter on a Chicago paper writes that "a shrill scream of publicity became a rancid roar." A critic on our college paper: "His singing style resembles someone having a painful bowel movement, a habit that would put a damper on many performers' acts." A candidate for the United States Senate: "The cement of this Union is in the heartblood of every American." A historian: "The American banking system of the '30s was haunted by an absence of public confidence" (the little ghost that wasn't there?). An economist: "The stockmarket snowballed to a boom." An English professor submitting a paper for publication: "The concept of team teaching impacted college teaching . . . ." And this "impact," she remarks, "will filter downward" and "will also circle back."

If such metaphorical incongruities are set side by side with effective use of metaphor, students will begin to understand a crucial—if paradoxical—fact about figurative language as used in ordinary prose. Good metaphor is tied to the literal, attached to it, as a kite is attached to a small boy. If a metaphor is not literally accurate and precise, it may not work.

The idea of *precision* itself presents difficulties in usage. One of my graduate students in composition is writing a dissertation on pigs; he is already publishing papers in his scientific field. He is trying to discover why pigs fight, hurt, and kill each other. He writes of a pig's *"microenvironment, a space all around the animal of no more than two feet."* I bet myself that when I turned the page I would find *macroenvironment.* And sure enough, there it was, along with a half-dozen other special terms, all of which were invented by pig specialists to make communication more precise. But *fake precision,* as I call such usages, does not do that. Instead it makes scientific papers harder to read for everyone—from pig professors to farmers.

Without exception, the students in English 302 have had direct experience with fake precision. Every academic discipline provides its examples. We look at a few in class, bearing in mind the words of the great geologist G. O. Smith, who wrote more than a half-century ago: ". . . I confess that I, too, have had the unhappy experience of stripping the technical words from what looked like a good-sized geological deduction only to find that the naked idea was rather small and not my own."[9]

V

The last two or three weeks of English 302 are devoted to those discussions that the course, in large part, is designed to examine. We start by looking at a few well-known writers to see how they employ words and grammatical techniques. It means something, for example, to learn that Hemingway uses ten expletive constructions in the first two pages of *A Farewell to Arms;* that Shakespeare uses *be* forms in profusion (of what value then is the ancient admonition to avoid *be* forms in favor of livelier "active verbs"?). And that Conrad combines colloquial words and solemn, stately terms in passages which employ an incredible range of grammatical forms.

Here at the end of the course, it is particularly important for students to combine the material on readability (Chapter 1) with everything they have so far learned. We analyze a single sentence in a paragraph context, trying for a complete understanding of the success or failure of the sentence. Here are several passages for analysis, each followed by an edited compilation of student comment. Except where noted, *sentence* refers to the italicized sentence that is the focus of discussion.

Passage One

The idea of Macbeth as a conscience-tormented man is a platitude as false as Macbeth himself. Macbeth has no conscience. His main concern throughout the play is that most selfish of all concerns: to get a good night's sleep. His invocation to sleep, while heartfelt, is perfectly conventional; sleep builds you up, enables you to start the day fresh. *Thus the virtue of having a good conscience is seen by him in terms of bodily hygiene, as if it were a Simmons mattress or an electric blanket.* Lady Macbeth shares these preoccupations. When he tells her he is going to see the witches, she remarks that he needs sleep. —*Mary McCarthy*[10]

The italicized sentence starts to fail when McCarthy shifts the rhetorical subject. Earlier, she placed the emphasis of the subject on Macbeth and his concerns. But at the beginning of the sentence in question, she emphasizes the abstraction *virtue*, which is not closely tied to the logic of the paragraph. After this mistake, the sentence begins to develop erratically. (Throughout the course, I have insisted that the common teacherly remark that the verb is the most important element in a sentence is wrong. If one must discuss relative importance, the subject-verb relation—*predication*—is the most important, with the subject second, and the verb third.)

To complete the predication and supply an agent, McCarthy stumbles along with *is seen by him* and pauses (one imagines), wondering how to continue. *In terms of* is the typical desperate ploy of a writer who must jump somehow across a hole in syntax. She lands uncertainly on *bodily hygiene*, and then slides out of control into metaphors of Simmons mattress and electric blanket that are ludicrously inappropriate. At the end of the sentence she clings to grammatical virtue by exploiting the subjunctive, thinking subconsciously, perhaps, that a hoity-toity form will rescue the whole bedraggled thing. In the next sentence she is firmly on her feet again and striding calmly along as if nothing amiss had occurred.

The sentence is a good example of what can happen even to a very good writer, as McCarthy generally is: lose your footing, and you may stagger and fall. Better to back up and start over. If she had continued the pattern of the first four sentences in the paragraph, she could have started properly: *Thus he sees a good conscience as no more than . . . .* And all would have been well.

Passage Two

That was when people had begun to feel really sorry for her. People in our town, remembering how Old Lady Wyatt, her great-aunt, had gone completely crazy at last, believed that the Griersons held themselves a little too high for what they really were. None of the young men were quite good enough for Miss Emily and such. *We had long thought of them as a tableau: Miss Emily a slender figure in white in the background, her father a spraddled silhouette in the foreground, his back to her and clutching a horsewhip, the two of them framed by the back-flung front door.* So when she got to be thirty and was still single, we were not pleased exactly, but vindicated; even with insanity in the family she wouldn't have turned down all of her chances if they had really materialized.—*William Faulkner*[11]

A Rose for Emily is told from a complex point of view that ultimately expresses the attitude of the town toward Miss Emily; thus the *we* at the beginning of the italicized sentence. Using the sentence-unit analysis, we note that Faulkner starts a sentence base that ends with the colon. *We* supplies viewpoint; *them* and *tableau* prepare us for material to come. The base is short and precise, with clearly defined predication.

The base is followed by four closers that explain and specify key words in the base. The first two closers contrast Miss Emily and her father; the third describes the father in more detail; the fourth sums up the first three and sharpens the image suggested by *tableau*. The parallelism of the first two closers is almost geometrically neat, although there is a hint of surprise in the participle *spraddled* (a partial metaphor involving *spread* and *straddle* that suggests at once truculence, drunkenness, and sexual posturing). The third closer is an absolute that concludes with half a participle, *clutching a horsewhip*. I say "half" because, in being distanced from *father* and also controlled by the absolute nature of *his back to her*, the phrase has lost some of its modificational bond. The fourth closer is also an absolute. It contains a standard participial modifier (starting with *framed*) and a remarkable participial compound in *back-flung*.

Why didn't Faulkner write: *framed by the front door which was flung back?* Probably because the more ordinary grammar of this phrase would not have provided the energy and metrical roughness of *báck-flúng front dóor*.

Once through the sentence, Faulkner slides easily into more ordinary grammar and rhetoric: *So when she got to be thirty and was still single, we were not pleased exactly . . . .*

Passage Three

By the end of March he [Thoreau] borrowed an axe from Alcott, cut down some white pine timber beside Walden Pond to frame a hut, and on Independence Day, which was highly propitious, he moved in and lived there alone for two years. *Watching and listening, studying, thinking, dreaming, attending to the varying moods of the pond, writing in his journals, trying the virtue of the great world outside by the simple truths of his secluded existence —all that brought his career to fruition.* Although he left the hut in 1847 and supported himself by surveying, pencil-making, and other homely crafts, he had found the path to a wise approach to life at Walden Pond, and from that time on he was a man whose destiny was in full view. Sometimes Thoreau seemed needlessly morose . . . .—*Brooks Atkinson*[12]

The italicized sentence represents a remarkable change in rhythm and expositional viewpoint from the sentence preceding. The first sentence emphasizes Thoreau; its final clause acts as the end of a periodic element that starts with *on Independence Day*. The italicized sentence begins with *-ing* words that help develop the actions implied in the previous main clause: *he moved in and lived there alone for two years*. The seven parallel structures in the sentence are unusual. They not only represent activities of different kinds, they also imply cause-and-effect, sequence of time, and classification of activities. Thoreau watches and listens; then he studies and dreams. *Attending to the varying moods of the pond* is partly a loose classification of previous activities. *Writing in his journals* is a result of these activities; *trying the virtue*, etc. is the reason for doing everything else, and also the climax of the series.

The grammar here is unusual. Until you get to the main clause, you don't know whether the *-ing* words are participles or gerunds. This ambiguity creates rhetorical tension and supplies suspense— how is the description going to end? We are surprised perhaps to see the sentence taking a turn after the dash that we had not expected. Wouldn't most writers start the main clause with *Thoreau* or *he?* By the time we finish, we know that the *-ing* words are meant to be gerunds, and we may well admire the writer both for his syntactical acrobatics and for his canniness in making the sentence unpredictable yet readable.

About half the class, however, raises an objection: "It isn't entirely readable. We read the final clause as *ALL that brought his career to fruition.* The opening *-ing* words confused us enough that we took *all* to be a pronoun subject with a delayed verb for predication, and *that brought his career to fruition* to be an adjective clause."

The students have raised a good point. There is something wrong with *that* in the final clause. How to fix it? They suggest omitting any possible sign of subordination: *all* this *brought* . . . or: *all these activities brought* . . . .

Students agree that the acrobatical sentence was worth discussing, and that the risks the writer took were worth taking. He packed an enormous amount of material into one sentence, and showed us how grammar and rhetoric can work well together—and also how one word wrongly used can pull down a painstakingly constructed edifice.

Passage Four

Alternative Methods of Energy Analysis

There are four basic ways to perform an energy analysis on an energy-producing system:

Process Analysis
Input-Output Analysis
Hybrid Analysis
Eco-energetic Analysis

Process Analysis. Under this method of energy analysis, the fabrication history of the system under examination is traced backward in time to its inception, when the raw materials from which the system is made are being mined from the earth. The direct use of energy is calculated at each step of fabrication while non-energy inputs (such as construction materials and capital equipment) are traced back until the energy used in their production can be calculated. This process continues until all direct and indirect energy inputs to the system can be calculated.

The passage was written by one of my graduate students in composition—I'll call him Smith. Smith has a degree in electrical engineering and is finishing law school this semester. The sample passage is part of a report he has written for a federally funded project. Our sample is taken from page 10 of his report.

My students notice two things early in our discussion. The first is that Smith is a victim of *fake precision*. He has been writing for nine pages on *energy analysis;* the term is in his heading and his lead sentence. Yet he unnecessarily repeats it in the italicized sentence. Furthermore, like many highly trained American specialists in various fields, he seems afraid to write something and move on. He must beat the thing to death. To write *system* is not enough; he must write *system under examination; traced backward* is insufficient; we must be told that we are tracing backward *in time*.

Editors usually complain of "redundancy" in discussing a sentence like this. Yet if you talk to someone who writes such stuff, you become aware of a motive behind the redundancy. The writer believes that to express ideas exactly and precisely he must say everything at once, and repetitively. He is afraid to leave anything out.

Other flaws in the sentence: the subject-verb relation is weak, *fabrication history is traced*. The sentence is needlessly nouny throughout. Smith is guilty of preposition piling: *under* method, *of* analysis, *of* system, *under* examination, *in* time, *to* inception, *from* which, *from* earth.

My students suggest a rewrite. "Shorten the opener; make the verb transitive; cut the fake precision; in fact, cut everything that in the context of the material can be omitted. Their edited sentence reads: *Using this method, we trace the history of fabrication back to the raw materials.*

Later I talked to Smith about the sentence, and he agreed that the edited version said what he wanted to say.

VI

It is very difficult to discuss the teaching of grammar, more difficult (it seems to me) than doing it. As a subject, grammar teaching is like an angry porcupine, all motion and sharp points. Wherever you grab it, you wish you had grabbed it somewhere else. My solution here has been to make a series of short grabs to keep the beast under control, and then to pray for good luck. Now that the enterprise is completed, we don't have a philosophy of grammar or pedagogy, but we may have the beginnings of both—and a whole skin.

Anyone who wishes to teach grammar, or install courses in it, should have a reasonable idea of what he wishes to accomplish. A course can emphasize grammatical theory, the naming of parts, questions of usage and propriety, issues in linguistics, the passing of objective tests. Or all of these and more.

But what is useful for one group of students may not be useful for another. Surely undergraduate English majors in a teaching program should learn some grammar, but should all ninth-graders in a school system study the subject? My wife Charlene is responsible for the English curriculum in a five-year junior high and high school. Her curriculum requires no formal English grammar. This is a college preparatory school in which every student must take one foreign language for at least four years and solid academic courses all the way through. Students go on to the best universities with no sense of grammatical loss. Students in the other local high schools all learn at least some formal grammar, although how useful their study is may be debatable.

I do not pretend that *English 302, Grammar and Usage*, is an exemplar for the profession. It is only one teacher's attempt to balance the needs of student, society, and discipline; to shape pedagogical materials so that truth about and in language can be reasonably well served. It is more a metaphor than a program.

I would be pleased to hear your views on how to corral the grammatical porcupine.

3 Here I Stand

How can I write anything? I just got here. I don't know where I am yet!
New Freshman

My new freshman was not lost as a person, just as a writer. It took him only a day or so to locate himself physically on our large campus. But almost two months passed before he was able to locate himself as a writer. At the beginning, he was a landlubber on a ship in a violent and stormy ocean, unable to keep his footing. He needed a place to stand that did not pitch about so much, a way to keep his bearings.

It is typical of the practiced writer that he creates priorities. First among these is to find ways to get out of heavy seas into calm water, in order to control his rhetorical ship. If nothing else, *he* will command the situation.

We can see how practiced writers do this by looking at several examples. Let us begin with Mark Twain. The passage is from *The Innocents Abroad:*

> It is hard to forget repulsive things. I remember yet how I ran off from school once, when I was a boy, and then, pretty late at night, concluded to climb into the window of my father's office and sleep on a lounge, because I had a delicacy about going home and getting thrashed. As I lay on the lounge and my eyes

grew accustomed to the darkness, I fancied I could see a long, dusky, shapeless thing stretched upon the floor. A cold shiver went through me. I turned my face to the wall. That did not answer. I was afraid that that thing would creep over and seize me in the dark. I turned back and stared at it for minutes and minutes—they seemed hours. It appeared to me that the lagging moonlight never, never would get to it. I turned to the wall and counted twenty, to pass the feverish time away. I looked—the pale square was nearer. I turned again and counted fifty—it was almost touching it. With desperate will I turned again and counted one hundred, and faced about, all in a tremble. A white human hand lay in the moonlight! Such an awful sinking at the heart—such a sudden gasp for breath! I felt —I cannot tell *what* I felt. When I recovered strength enough, I faced the wall again. But no boy could have remained so, with that mysterious hand behind him. I counted again, and looked —the most of a naked arm was exposed. I put my hands over my eyes and counted till I could stand it no longer, and then—the pallid face of a man was there, with the corners of the mouth drawn down, and the eyes fixed and glassy in death! I raised to a sitting posture and glowered on that corpse till the light crept down the bare breast,—line by line—inch by inch—past the nipple,—and then it disclosed a ghastly stab![1]

One is reminded here of Twain the actor, standing before an eager audience. As stage prop, the ever-present cigar. He drawls his lines, pausing to let the images develop and fix themselves in the mind of the listener. The sentences are constructed to allow for one of Twain's great devices as an actor, the pause:

> I put my hands over my eyes and counted till I could stand it no longer *pause* and then *pause* the pallid face of a man was there *pause* with the corners of the mouth drawn down *pause* and the eyes fixed and glassy in death!

When dealing with passages like this, the temptation is to slide into a discussion of style. Twain, we say, writes in the loose and cumulative rather than the balanced mode, adding rather than coordinating syntactic elements. True enough. But what lies behind the mode and certain decisions to use it? What helps to shape the "style," whatever we mean by that term? Agreement on its meanings are hard to come by. I once chaired a national panel created for the purpose of discussing style, and we panelists could never agree on what our subject was.

Behind a style is, of course, a personality. And while one may choose to adopt a style, at the same time the style insists on adopting him. A witty writer, for example, has only so many syntactic options for expressing wit. Yet it is useful to observe that writers can be equally witty in loose and balanced styles (for example, Mark Twain in the loose; George Bernard Shaw in the balanced). Also influencing one's style is a culture and its literary influences—all of those patterns and habits that help shape one's way of looking at the world.

But let us resist, at least for the moment, the temptation to analyze style. Rather, what might interest us is how a writer decides to view his audience (or *reader*), himself, and his argument. This is the "rhetorical problem" that Wayne Booth speaks of in his famous article, "The Rhetorical Stance."[2] Booth believes that one cannot compose successful pieces of writing until he knows—and here I employ my own phrasing—*where he stands.*

In most of Twain's nonfiction, you get the impression of the actor standing on stage. His sentences are full of the nuances and shadings required by the performer: here a gesture, there a pause, now a phrase placed to anticipate the reaction of the audience, which listens. The transaction is oral; Twain was a master of the colloquial. To read him is to listen to a man speaking.

The issues of stance—where, how, and why the writer takes his stand—are complex and difficult. Cause and effect chase each other and change places. But we can learn from other examples. Here is a very different writer from Twain, Norman Mailer:

> McCarthy joined in the laughter. Hard was his face, hard as the bones and scourged flesh of incorruptibility, hard as the cold stone floor of a monastery in the North Woods at five in the morning. The reporter leaned forward to talk into his ear. "You see, sir," he said, "the tragedy of the whole business is that you should never have had to run for President. You would have been perfect for the Cabinet." A keen look back from McCarthy's eye gave the sanction to continue. "Yessir," said the reporter, "You'd have made a perfect chief for the F.B.I.!" and they looked

at each other and McCarthy smiled and said, "Of course, you're absolutely right."

The reporter looked across the table into one of the hardest, cleanest expressions he had ever seen, all the subtle hints of puffiness and doubt sometimes visible in the Senator's expression now gone, no, the face that looked back belonged to a tough man, tough as the harder alloys of steel, a merciless face and very just, the sort of black Irish face which could have belonged to one of the hanging judges in a true court of Heaven, or to the proper commissioner of a police force too honest ever to have existed.[3]

Mailer has never been accused of having a small ego. Yet in this passage describing Senator Eugene McCarthy as a presidential candidate, he seems at first glance modest enough. He even withdraws himself into the anonymity of the third person, "the reporter." But the withdrawal is thoroughly deceptive and actually a trick of stance.

While the argument is partly about McCarthy, it is more about Mailer. The wording, syntax, and tone draw attention to themselves and ultimately to the creator, "the reporter." There are repetitious inversions: "Hard was his face, hard as the bones . . . hard as the cold stone floor . . . ." There is the long, finely wrought sentence that makes up the whole third paragraph, with its novelistic piece of character description added by way of interpretation: ". . . no, the face that looked back belonged to a tough man . . . ." There are the vivid and consistent metaphors: "hard as the cold stone floor," "tough as the harder alloys of steel," "one of the hardest, cleanest, expressions he had ever seen . . . ."

All this, you may say, is a matter of style. And so it partly is. Yet behind the stylistic devices is Mailer the puppet master, pulling strings. He creates his own role; his argument is really about himself and what he believes to be his delicate blend of political wisdom and literary necromancy. Look at what I can perceive behind appearance, he seems to say. Even more, look at what I can *do* with the art at my command.

The passage fairly vibrates with Mailer's creative energy. The tone is poetic, vigorous, brassy, and self-confident—not to say self-conscious. The adopted role of anonymity should not fool most readers, many of whom will be aware that behind the mask of the reporter is Norman Mailer, proud word-magician and professional celebrity-watcher. Thus his seeming modesty turns into a kind of immodesty; the adopted stance plays against the very words, sentences, and tone of the writing; and the whole passage moves dangerously close to unconscious burlesque. Yet paradoxically, for many readers, it is persuasive and successful.

For our next example, we move back 120 years. The passage is from a letter to *The Times* (London, February 24, 1858):

Now, what if I am a prostitute, what business has society to abuse me? Have I received any favours at the hands of society? If I am a hideous cancer in society, are not the causes of the disease to be sought in the rottenness of the carcass? Am I not its legitimate child; no bastard, Sir? Why does my unnatural parent repudiate me, and what has society ever done for me, that I should do anything for it, and what have I ever done against society that it should drive me into a corner and crush me to the earth? I have neither stolen (at least since I was a child), nor murdered, nor defrauded. I earn my money and pay my way, and try to do good with it, according to my ideas of good. . . . I do not use bad language. I do not offend the public eye by open indecencies. I go to the Opera, I go to Almack's, I go to the theatres, I go to quiet, well-conducted casinos, I go to all the places of public amusement, behaving myself with as much propriety as society can exact. I pay business visits to my tradespeople, the most fashionable of the Westend. My milliners, my silk-mercers, my bootmakers, know, all of them, who I am and how I live, and they solicit my patronage as earnestly and cringingly as if I were Madam, the Lady of the right rev. patron of the Society for the Suppression of Vice. They find my money as good and my pay better (for we are robbed on every hand) than that of Madam, my Lady; and, if all the circumstances and conditions of our lives had been reversed, would Madam, my Lady, have done better or been better than I?[4]

One line of the argument is clear enough. It might be expressed in the old popular song: "You made me what I am today—I hope you're satisfied!" Also clear is the intended audience—Society, or at least that portion of it which strives to crush what it considers immoral. These emphases are sufficiently usual. Somewhat unusual is the intensity with which the writer plays her chosen role. She may not be Virtue, but she is certainly one who habitually piles virtue upon virtue.

She does not murder, steal, or defraud. She pays her own way with her (earned) money, and even tries to do good with it—adding, with delectable modesty, "according to my ideas of good." If her ideas of good are faulty, without question society (which has failed in its obligation to educate her) is to blame. She is not indecent; she goes to all the best places; and the Victorian reader must be impressed to learn that her credit is as good as any lady's in society. Her repeated references to solvency can be no accident. Nor is it any accident that she places the economic transaction in a position of emphasis, while neglecting to mention how the money was earned.

This writer stands before us as a superior being: industrious, independent, courageous. She turns the Victorian exemplar upside down, creating virtue out of vice while also creating a rhetorical role as consciously as ever did Disraeli, Shaw, or Churchill. Her role has its own tone of voice. Yet *tone* is itself an effect of certain causes, among them how the writer sees himself in relation to his argument and audience. Every writer of ability has available a multiplicity of legitimate roles that are peculiarly his. They may vary according to time, place, and situation. To a certain extent, he can shape them as he will. And it is this *shaping* that plays so important a part in the success and failure of compositions.

In recent years, theorists have written volumes on topics they consider important in analyzing and producing compositions. At one time or another, they have asked us to consider as primary *semantics, syntax, prewriting* (or, more formally, *heuristics), purpose, structure* of arguments, *"efficiency"* of prose.

Without question, one can study such matters and learn a great deal. But I suspect that if one thing is fundamental in the art and craft of composing, it is the question of stance. The writer asks himself: Who am I? Who is the reader? What is my point?—*now*. Not yesterday or tomorrow, but at this moment. One of the paradoxes of the effective composition, however, is that if it truly works for the moment for this generation of readers, it may work for other generations as well. The first-rate composition has a certain firmness in both material and outline, a genuine durability. The second-rate lacks this. It may, as we all know, lack other things—an ethical sense, for instance.

Let me provide an example of a composition that is worse than second-rate. I know because I wrote it.

I had started to write an introduction to a short book on certain developments in using and teaching English. In the middle of the second page of the introduction, I had just finished quoting the black minister and politician Jessie Jackson on what he called "a push for excellence" in teaching the language. Jackson was calling for higher standards. I continued:

To live a political or religious life, in the best ethical sense, is to judge matters according to a standard outside oneself. Based on history and experience, such a standard is continually being created by civilized people, the skeptics and libertarians of friendly persuasion. But there are fewer civilized every year. Our institutions crank out instead the intellectual—that *true believer* forever hunting for the perfect social, political, legal, educational, or economic form to pour his inchoate religious feelings into . . . .

Uneducated, and sometimes barely literate, the intellectual is paradoxically a man of words. For him, words *are* reality. In scholarship, he tends to form his premises through the use of slogans. In thinking about the public schools, he will build castles of conjecture, which he insists are as firm as stone and concrete, on a base of words like *integration, bussing,* and *racism.* When he writes textbooks on language and language theory he stays comfortably in his office, writing pithy mottoes, like *All usage is relative,* for those who automatically agree with him. A high school English teacher in Kansas told me: "Those Doctors of Education in the central office have lost touch with reality. We're down here with real students and real problems, and they are up in the clouds producing expensively printed pamphlets called *Education for the Eighties.*"

It is an unspoken tenet in the intellectual's religion that problems must never be identified by going to look at them or be discussed according to accepted standards. This partly accounts for his continually inventing "victims of society" by the neat device of changing his economic, social, and educational norms from day to day. As soon as he tires of exploiting one victim, he invents another until everyone in America is a victim of everyone else, leading to the sort of chaos in which the intellectual works best: people at each other's throats. The Doctor of Education does not go to the ninth-grade class to identify problems of English teaching because to identify or define them according to a recognized standard would mean that he might be held responsible for solving them. And it is necessary to his very existence that he never solve a problem—it could put the man of words out of business.

Here is the reason why our problems with American English —in the schools, the "media," and elsewhere—are not being effectively dealt with . . . .

Why is my composition bad? Looking back, I can now see all three elements of stance going out of control—almost at the same time. I forgot that I was introducing a book. Instead of telling the reader what the book was about, I was starting an argument that the reader was not ready for. The intellectual—whoever he may be—was not my true subject anyway.

About the same time, I lost a clear definition of myself as creator of the argument. The writer of these introductory paragraphs was supposed to be cool and somewhat objective. The writer who suddenly charges into the composition is laying about him with a broadsword, and woe to anybody within range. He is going to pull up in a minute, puffing and blowing, and wonder where everybody went to. The readers have long since departed (the writer forgot about them). In fact, some of them are those intellectuals the writer has been thumping with such glee. It is perilous to all but a genius to insult readers, a fact the writer pointed out to himself after he had cooled off.

In these paragraphs, I had unquestionably taken a stand—but inconsistently, inharmoniously, and to poor effect. The next day I simply ripped up the whole affair and started over: put on a new face, got a new argument, and tacked a new description of the reader above my desk. But in my heart of my hearts I did not take back what I had said about the intellectual; for it was true, I thought, as much as anything said about human beings is true. It fit the facts. It fit my prejudices. Yet it must be admitted that the truth of an argument, while of major importance, can be irrelevant. If readers won't read you with at least some sympathy, you might as well never write.

It is usually easy to point out where the experienced writer has gone wrong. He has enough training that he seldom goes entirely wrong. He won't write an incoherent argument while at the same time creating unparsable sentences, bad spelling, faulty punctuation, misleading grammar, and weird idioms. The untrained student, however, finds himself in a different situation. For him, writing can be a disaster in every way. Once he finishes a composition, it often seems disastrously unworkable, like a great ugly blob of concrete that has suddenly appeared and hardened on one's driveway.

We can hack away at the student's blob with various hammers and chisels—one labelled *grammar*, one labelled *word choice*, and so on. But perhaps it would be better to hire someone to haul it away so the student can start over. Here is where the idea of stance can help. We ask: what effect can a well chosen stance have on a piece of writing *before* it is written?

To begin answering the question, we take an unsuccessful paragraph discussing the choice of a class project in a college course called Environment and Man. The sentences are numbered for later discussion.

(1) The availability of time is an important factor in the project choice. (2) Substantial progress should be made towards the solution of the chosen problem by the end of the class' semester. (3) In view of this, a project should not require extensive and time-consuming library research. (4) The major portion of the semester should be spent in the field working towards discovering practical solutions to current environmental deficiencies.

Nearly everything that can go wrong with a piece of writing went wrong with this paragraph. Its point is fuzzy; the word choice is general and abstract (or plainly wrong); the sentences are clumsy and constipated; the paragraph "lead" is so vague that it gives the writer no help in organizing his materials. The remaining sentences appear to be thrown together like marbles in a bag.

In talking with the student, I suggested that he keep his basic idea for the paragraph but ask these three questions before rewriting:

1. Who is he in this paragraph—a student in the class? A reporter on the school paper? The teacher of the course? A

taxpayer? (The paragraph is written from no particular
viewpoint, as though the writer were a disembodied voice
hanging in midair.)
2. Who does he want to read his work—the whole student body?
His parents? His instructor? The dean of the college?
3. What does he want the reader to believe or do?

After answering these questions, the student created a new
stance, one which encouraged him to write a more exact and
readable paragraph. Writing now as a member of the class in
Environment and Man, he addresses the other members:

(1) In choosing a problem for our project, we must remember
that we have only four months' time. (2) By the end of the third
month, we should not only have identified the problem, but also
have started on a practical solution to it. (3) We should avoid
problems which require extensive research in the library or a
lot of travel around the state (all members of the class are
full-time students in the University, and ten of us have part-
time jobs). (4) Probably, most of us will have to limit our library
research to a few basic books or magazines and our field work to
Champaign County.

The student's rewrite—which is noticeably better than the
original—is not primarily the result of standard teaching techniques. By this I mean that the improved organization, wording,
style, and content in the second version are not basically the result of
studying these arts of composition directly. Rather, they are the
result of improving the stance and specifying what might be called
the "rhetorical situation."

Wayne Booth opened his article on stance with this description
of such a situation:

Last fall I had an advanced graduate student, bright, energetic,
well-informed, whose papers were almost unreadable. He
managed to be pretentious, dull, and disorganized in his paper
on *Emma*, and pretentious, dull, and disorganized on *Madame
Bovary*. On *The Golden Bowl* he was all these and obscure as
well. Then one day, toward the end of the term, he cornered me
after class and said, "You know, I think you were all wrong

about Robbe-Grillet's *Jealousy* today." We didn't have time to discuss his objections, so I suggested that he write me a note about them. Five hours later I found in my faculty mail box a four-page polemic, unpretentious, stimulating, organized, convincing. Here was a man who had taught freshman composition for several years and who was incapable of committing any of the more obvious errors that we think of as characteristic of bad writing. Yet he could not write a decent sentence, paragraph, or paper until his rhetorical problem was solved—until, that is, he found a definition of his audience, his argument, and his own proper tone of voice.[5]

It is worth mentioning that Booth makes no special note of the fact that his inept graduate student was led into improving his stance by conditions created mainly by Booth himself. He had made certain provocative remarks about Robbe-Grillet's *Jealousy*. The student took issue with Booth, who promptly suggested that the young man make his disagreement clear in writing. The *rhetorical situation* was clearly outlined, if somewhat unconsciously, by two persons, both of whom were looking at the same set of "facts" and interpretations. A fairly well-defined situation was created here, by an interaction of ideas and people (plus a request for a persuasive statement), which enabled the student to write a successful paper.

Like Booth, I had helped set up a rhetorical situation. I had asked certain questions of the student: "What is your interest in this class?" "What is your opinion of the project?" "Are you trying to get someone, or a group, to believe or to do something?—What?" By asking such questions, I was creating *and specifying* the rhetorical situation and suggesting the possibility of several stances the student might reasonably take.

These remarks lead me to a parenthesis about the way we often teach our composition courses in the United States. In the non-academic world, people almost never write without a pretty definite rhetorical situation. The lawyer writes an opinion because a legal problem exists, and he is required to comment on it. As part of her job, an accountant writes a report to the directors of a bank. A customer writes a complaint about service to the head office of a grocery chain. The manager of a beer bar writes a set of directions to his part-time help, explaining how they are to change kegs, fill glasses, and so on.

Even given the fact that their rhetorical situations are created in part for them, it is often difficult for the lawyer, accountant, customer, and bar manager to write their communications success-fully. Think how difficult it is for our students, when we give them no situations to spur them on, but ask merely that they produce a certain amount of writing at thus-and-such a time. My point is that managing rhetorical stance properly is more than just the student's responsibility. As teachers, we are at times also responsible for creating real-world situations to which students may respond, and in which they can create useful stances. This can mean writing assignments that may run as long as a full-typed page, assignments that set up situations and suggest problems to be analyzed, solved, and communicated to a reader.

For some years now, I have been talking to teachers, both formally and informally, about the uses of stance in compositions. I usually defend the value of teaching it and, as might be imagined, get some pretty sharp questions from skeptical teachers. Some of the more interesting questions or objections are worthy of discussion here.

Question One: Isn't stance simply a modern version of certain devices in classical rhetoric?

It can be answered that most of the useful ideas in modern rhetoric are no more than modern versions of old ideas. (The ancients seem to have thought of everything.) For instance, the use of stance is certainly implied in the practice, in ancient schools, of teaching the *controversiae*, manufactured legal cases on which students composed arguments. The case would be described, and the student would imagine it being presented before the court as he developed the issues and took a particular side.[6] As Edward Corbett remarked in the Preface to his *Classical Rhetoric for the Modern Student*, "the methods of learning how to write have not changed very much since the Sophists first set up their schools of rhetoric in the fifth-century Athens."[7]

Question Two: Is stance widely useful in all parts of the composition course? For example, can one use it when teaching description or the literary paper?

I am not sure about description, because I usually don't teach it as such. That is, I seldom assign a description as an entire paper or theme. Apart from composition courses, descriptions are usually written to support an argument. So I tend, rightly or wrongly, to teach description as a form of evidence. So far as literary papers (and other special assignments) are concerned, it appears that a well-chosen stance helps the young writer a good deal. I remember when as an undergraduate I first read Twain's *Mysterious Stranger*, that the novel seemed to me an odd combination of greatness and absurdity: great as narrative and polemic, absurd as a philosophical or religious statement. Certain class members disagreed with me, and so I wrote my brief course paper as if it were a response to their viewpoint. Years later, when I looked over my youthful papers, I thought that the Twain job was the only one worth much, mainly because it wasn't written in that rhetorical vacuum created by so many literary assignments—"Analyze the symbolism of *Leaves of Grass*" ("analyze" for whom, and for what reason?).

Question Three: Even if you're right about the value of teaching stance in most parts of the composition course, can you prove that stance makes much difference in a student's word choice, sentence structure, and other matters?

It is obviously true that we teachers can ignore stance and work with our students on content, organization, word choice, sentence structure, and logic. With the textbooks available, we can teach these matters directly and improve a student's writing. And I am all for doing just that. Much good teaching is no more than slogging through the necessary drills and techniques. But when we limit our work to drills, we are to a certain extent treating symptoms rather than causes.

When the student has no particular *rhetorical situation* to encourage him to communicate, when he does not know who he is in the situation or what his point in writing is, and when he has no reader in mind, the fuzziness of the whole thing affects him in fundamental ways. He becomes more vague, disorganized, and unconvincing than he might ordinarily be. Compare the two versions of my student's paragraph, particularly the beginning sentences. After he found a better stance, the useless subject phrase *availability of time* simply disappears. Then he is able to get started on his paragraph more clearly and gracefully.

And since he has made a good start, he finds it easy to continue. The weak passive in the first version (sentence 2) turns into an SVO: "*We . . . identified the problem.*" Organizationally, he is now able to tie his sentences together:

1. *We* must remember that . . .
2. *We* . . . identified the problem . . .

3. *We* should avoid problems . . .
4. Most of *us* will have to limit . . . .

It is no accident that he is now writing tight SVO patterns, for (given the stance he has chosen) he is dealing with an "action situation." And since he is trying to get his reader to do something, he has improved the content of his message and become more specific (sentence 3). It is also no accident that the wording of the rewrite has lost much of its empty jargon. The original version could have been written by a machine, the phrases being "tacked together," as Orwell put it in "Politics and the English Language," "like the sections of a prefabricated hen house." The second version may have its faults, but at least it is human and is written in a human language.

Question Four: Even if what you have said so far is true, aren't you pumping up a small idea into a big one? That is, isn't the question of stance no more than deciding why you write, for whom you write, and how you want to appear to the reader?

It is true that most of us who teach writing have pet notions that we would be wise—now and again—to give a rest to. Yet the reality of my own experience always leads me back to the issues involved in stance. *"No more than deciding . . ."*? Of the students you teach, how many in their papers regularly come to grips with the basic elements of writer's *role, point, reader?* For whom are their weekly themes written? Do their research papers have a definite reader or type of reader in mind? (And I don't mean the instructor.) Do they appear in their own papers as personalities, even as neutral ones adopting a neutral role? Do they know how to get a point across?

After they graduate, students will have to come to grips with questions like these. Many years ago I succeeded as a young engineer not because I was a good one—I wasn't—but because I followed the advice of a wise geophysicist who told me:

Your reports are too pompous—too full of "Hey Ma, look—I'm doing Science." Take off your mortar board and put on an ordinary cap. And direct your reports toward your real readers —not just to the division head they're nominally addressed to; he is only a technician. Direct them also to the guy who spends the money, the accountant-vice president in Chicago. Satisfy both of *them,* and you're on your way. And, finally, put the point of your reports in two places. State it at the beginning, and then restate it at the end. Most people don't read the middle of a report unless they find something at the beginning or the end that makes them want to read the middle.

It was partly by following his advice on writing that I survived as an engineer; far better scientists fell by the wayside. Later, I worked full-time as an editor of scullery prose. Scullery editors help to produce the millions of words necessary to keep American life going—to help repair machinery, run businesses, make political life possible. One day, I'd edit a piece on fixing a faulty transmission; the next I would ghostwrite a speech for an Air Force colonel. Again, stance was always at the top of those problems that had to be solved for the transmission to be fixed or for the colonel to win his military argument.

Because I like to branch out as a teacher, in the last decade I have taught about thirty sections of business writing. The students are juniors and seniors and among the brightest in the university; our Commerce College has very high entrance requirements. We teachers spend much of our time in the business writing course trying to break students of bad writing habits and training them in good ones. If you visit classes, you hear the same admonitions:

"Who *are* you in this letter; are you speaking for management or somebody else?"
"Your memo runs two pages. What's the *point* of it?"
"This Coding Regulation could be understood only by lawyers. But you claim that it is written for householders. Will they even read past the first page?"
"You've buried the point in the middle of the fourth paragraph. Why?"

Teachers in our Business and Technical Writing Division give workshops throughout much of the Midwest. We talk to scientists, journalists, lawyers, accountants, engineers, federal and state employees, managers at various levels. We always work with samples of their own writing problems. They usually want to talk about grammar. They are fixated on the subject, although they don't know a clause from a phrase. If you inspect their writing as something created in the genuine context of their lives, you find—as you would imagine—more than one problem with it. But a major problem, and the one that causes many of the others, lies in their failure to define an appropriate stance. Consider these examples from my files:

1. *RESTRICTED FIRE USE AREA.* A sign in a national park. Can you light a fire in this area? Why or why not? Fire *"restricted* to whom"? Or what? How about a small fire carefully built? Who wrote these words and on whose authority?

2. *Accurate and thorough documentation of personnel decisions is an absolute necessity when justifying decisions.* The person who got this message did not even know it was directed to him, did not recognize any authority behind it, and (most important) did not act on it.

3. *Children who become the "parents" of the pet may develop a more realistic view of their own parents and parenting functions, not only nurturant but disciplinary in nature.* This is the final paragraph from an article in a popular and carefully edited national magazine. Who is talking to whom here, and to what end?

Until about ten years ago, my own teacherly reaction to such writing was the typical one—*Good God, the jargon!* This reaction would be followed by an analysis of gobbledygook, abstraction, and fad terms, and my admonition to the writers to go and sin no more. But a decade of talking to the writers who produce such *garblish* has changed my mind.

I've come to believe that while a love for phony abstraction does lie behind some bad writing, more important is the writers' fear of standing out in the open. Each of the messages reproduced above is written by a typical educated American, but one who is desperately afraid of appearing in the message as a human being speaking. And who made them afraid? We did—you and I, the English teachers of the nation. For the past five years, Charlene and I have been talking to high school and college English teachers about instruction in composition. In 1976-77, we travelled 18,000 miles around the United States looking at real students and their themes, and discussing pedagogical issues with teachers. In a smaller sample of universities, we did the same thing.

Our conclusion was that the kind of writing represented in samples 1 through 3 is being *taught* to students, through their teachers' insistence that writing be done by and for nobody. In *What's Happening to American English*, we asked the question, "Why are high school students producing vague, abstract, jargony English?" Our answer:

> Because they are being trained to produce it as calculatedly as one might teach one's dog to roll over and play dead. Behind the dull abstraction and the occasional narcotic metaphor is the guiding hand of teachers who believe that the worst words in the language are those that come trippingly to the tongue. Their first linguistic commandment is, Thou shalt not commit the colloquial. No piece of writing should ever sound like human speech; if it does, ruthlessly strike it out. Their second commandment is, Thou shalt never admit to being part of what you write. It was not you who wrote this composition; rather, you caused it to be written. Therefore, never use the word *I;* for if you do, people may suspect that you had an intimate connection with the thing.[8]

If you want to test my theory that we may be deliberately teaching students to write stance-less prose, try an experiment like the one I conducted while doing a final version of this chapter. I have a group of intelligent and well-motivated advanced undergraduates in an eight o'clock elective grammar class. (Put *elective, grammar,* and *eight o'clock* together, and you have an idea of their motivation for learning.)

After six weeks of discussion of grammar and writing, but before our units on readability and editing, I asked them to rewrite this sentence, which you may remember from Chapter 1:

> Parental endeavors in regard to education suggest an ambitious drive toward self-improvement and they are presenting an interest in upward mobility.

Here are five of their typical rewrites:

> An ambitious drive for self-improvement and an interest in upward mobility make education a parental endeavor.

Self-improvement and upward mobility are parental endeavors in an ambitious drive to education.

An ambitious drive toward self-improvement and an interest in upward mobility are trends in parental endeavors in education.

In regards to education, parental endeavors suggest an ambitious drive toward self-improvement and present an interest in upward mobility.

Parental endeavors in education suggest an ambitious drive toward self-improvement and an interest in upward mobility.

All of these student writers have had twelve years of public school English and also the university freshman English course. But not one of them thought to ask the obvious questions about the stance of the original message.

You will observe that my students' rewrites are not significantly different from my samples 1 through 3, all of which—to repeat—were written by either advanced college students or college graduates. When you talk to such graduates and tell them: "Put yourself, your reader, and your point into the message," you get a wonderful reaction. They begin to squirm, look away, become physically uncomfortable. We can't do *that*, they say. But they don't want to talk about why it can't be done. The very idea of *I* and *you* in a message is nearly obscene to them.

In 1967, F. Peter Woodford, editor of the *Journal of Lipid Research*, wrote in the prestigious journal *Science:*

When science students enter graduate school they often write with admirable directness and clarity of purpose, like this:

In order to determine the molecular size and shape of A and B, I measured their sedimentation and diffusion constants. The results are given in Table 1. They show that A is a roughly spherical molecule of molecular weight 36,000. The molecular weight of B remains uncertain since the sample seems to be impure. This is being further investigated.

Two years later, these same students' writing is verbose, pompous, full of fashionable circumlocutions as well as dangling constructions, and painfully polysyllabic, like this:

In order to evaluate the possible significance of certain molecular parameters at the subcellular level, and to shed light on the conceivable role of structural configuration in spatial relationships of intracellular macromolecules, an integrated approach [see 1] to the problem of cell diffusivity has been devised and developed.

Dr. Woodford commented on the issues behind this kind of stanceless prose:

> In teaching scientific writing it is not difficult to point out the absurdity of the bombastic phraseology discussed above, and to teach students to simplify their writing and make it direct and vigorous. But these stylistic considerations only scratch the surface of what is really at fault in many scientific articles. I am appalled by the frequent publication of papers that describe most minutely what experiments were done, and how, but with no hint of why, or what they mean. Cast thy data upon the waters, the authors seem to think, and they will come back interpreted.[9]

To return to the question asked several pages back: are we discussing in this essay only the "small idea" of "deciding why you write, for whom you write, and how you want to appear to the reader"?

Perhaps the small idea is much bigger than we teachers might like to admit. If you read good nonfiction writing and talk to the professionals who wrote it, you discover certain similarities of purpose and strategy. For example, like Woodford, they are greatly interested in the point of a message: *What does all this mean?* And they are unusually sensitive to the reader's responses, reacting seismographically to the slightest possible change in the reader's attitude. A raised eyebrow, as it were, produces an adjustment on the writer's part: *Oh, you don't quite get that? I'll rephrase, and add a small definition.*

What I wish, finally, to suggest is that while there are many methods of teaching writing successfully, some are more fundamental than others. We certainly should not condemn any that have good lasting results. The evidence found in specimens of work done by professional writers indicates that they instinctively search for a place to stand. As craftsmen, they are uncomfortable unless they find a platform upon which to present themselves (sometimes in strange guises!), and from which they can launch an argument at readers they have identified.

What the professional does instinctively, the inexperienced writer can be taught to do.

4 Some Techniques of Organization

There is no body of regulations by which the essayist or speech writer may determine what element belongs where. An essay, as a structure, is successful if it always moves, or gives the illusion of moving, toward its conclusion.
William Brandt, *The Rhetoric of Argumentation*[1]

I dealt indirectly with the problem of organization in the last essay. If a writer creates an appropriate stance, he may find that organization partly takes care of itself. We will suppose that he understands what he is to prove (and to whom), and that he has chosen the vantage point from which he intends to argue the case. All this will suggest—even create—a certain organization. Yet there is obviously more to be said on the topic of organizing, more indeed than most textbooks can say, or wish to.

Textbooks customarily handle the problem of organization by teaching the student *schemata* which, if followed, promise to take him from point A to point Z. But schemata have a habit of being at cross purposes with the basic elements of communication—subject, thesis, reader. In such cases an essay begins to fight with itself, and occasionally ends by gnawing off its own tail or leg. Schemata are useful, however—and sometimes they are perfect for the occasion. Yet even with their help, the essays produced by many writers lie inert and shapeless, like so many pounds of wet mud shovelled on the page.

Brandt's observation quoted in my epigraph—that an essay should move toward a conclusion—is true enough. The question is: how does the writer *produce* such movement of ideas? By no means can it always be produced by injections of that textbook favorite, the *thesis statement* (hereafter simply called *thesis*). Now let me confess to some hypocrisy. I am responsible for a chapter on thesis in a certain textbook, now in its third edition. I am not ashamed of this chapter, although I admit to feeling ambiguous about it. Teachers who use the book usually don't object to it. I teach the chapter, or something like it, to my own students. Yet I'll have to admit that there is something oddly off-center about the idea of a thesis crammed into one sentence: it often seems mechanical, excessively neat, and (most of all) premature.

How many of us really use a firm thesis to start a piece of writing? It may be easy enough to start with one if you have all the evidence on a topic and you are producing an argument that can be organized mechanically, as if you were using a rhetorical cooky-cutter. For example, a thesis of fact: *The seismographic evidence shows that there are no anticlinal closures worth investigating in the Ordovician rocks in XYZ Prospect.* Or a thesis of action: *We must abolish the advanced composition course for freshmen because the students taking the course need more basic training and should take the regular course.*

In arguments of this nature, you take a run at your evidence, make the appropriate inductive leap to a conclusion, state it with a one-sentence thesis, and lo—the cooky-cutter can be pressed into service. The argument organizes itself.

But many arguments must be formed out of more intractable materials, which is why a thesis can be premature. For example, I tried three or four theses for this chapter, none of which worked. The thesis pointed one way, the chapter insisted on going in another. So I started writing the chapter to see where it wanted to go. It trotted along the road nicely for a while, and then headed abruptly for the grass. I outlined the chapter up to the grass. The outline suggested that my chapter was acting like a large undisciplined dog; only a choker chain would keep it off the grass. It kept wanting to be a chapter in a textbook, while I wanted it to move on to better things. Scrap one outline, thesis, and chapter.

At this point, I remembered my wife Charlene's experience with a graduate student who had a terrible time starting to write. He was a high school principal on sabbatical; his dissertation subject was educational administration. He showed Charlene a dozen pages of false starts. She read them and asked: "How many subjects have you got here?" The student said: "That's part of the problem. I've got so much to say that I don't know where to begin. If I could just get started. . . ." Charlene pointed to the back of the room. Along the wall was a line of coat hooks, and his coat was hanging on one of them.

"Look at your coat," Charlene said. "When you came in, you didn't throw your coat at the wall and hope it would miraculously stay up there. You hung it high and dry on a hook. You're trying to throw your paper at a rhetorical wall, hoping it will stay there; but your subject keeps falling down in a heap. Try some hooks. For example: *Why school principals fail.* The hook is provided in the words *why* and *fail.* As you write, keep hanging your ideas on those two words." Charlene told him of other possible hooks in these titles:

The *Successful* Principal *Listens*
How a *Good* Principal *Prepares*
A *Good* Principal is *Lucky*
The *Principal* and Town *Politics*
Should *You* be a School *Principal?*

The last title has the hooks *you* and *principal,* with the added control of a question; the point of that chapter is implied in the question, which can be answered in several ways. Charlene told the student: "Now provide another hook for your paper, something like the phrase *qualities of leadership.* In your introduction to the paper, start to answer the question in the title by telling readers that they can be *successful school principals* if they have certain *qualities of leadership.*"

I'm not sure why the hook device works as well as it does. (By *well,* I mean that it is helpful more than half of the time, which sets something of a record for pedagogical devices.) Perhaps it's the vividness of the metaphor—don't throw your ideas at a wall and expect them to stick. And don't try to hang your ideas on too many hooks; they will just fall down. Pick one or two (sometimes three) firm, well-defined hooks, and hang your rhetorical coat on them.

Perhaps, too, the hook supplies some flexibility that a thesis lacks. When I've worked in writing labs, I have often noticed students staring mournfully at a neat single page of thesis *cum* outline, the very air around their heads sodden with misery. In educationist cant, they are suffering writer's block. They can often be unblocked by a suggestion like this: "Take a word or phrase in your thesis—*ambition*, for instance, or *coaching error*—and just start writing. Don't think, write!" I once wrote *smothering mother* on a student's outline and said: *Push that pencil, push!* At the end of the hour I had to push her out of the room.

Perhaps, finally, the hook as a word or phrase releases emotional energy that tends to be suppressed by the more logical and rather grim-looking thesis. Maybe we should label the hook (with apologies to James McCrimmon) *free-writing with a purpose*.

As that expression suggests, the hook crosses several leaky barriers in the so-called writing process. I am treating it here as an organizational device. It forces the writer to group his ideas around a certain point or points; it suggests that he move toward certain goals. For the writer who has trouble starting, the hook forces him to concentrate on certain things to the possible exclusion of others. Here's a list of my scratch-paper hooks for parts of this chapter:

Organization

Techniques of organization
Not covered in some textbooks
No set rules of organization
Writer's block
"Movement of ideas"
Hooks
Hooks for reader and writer
Writer's contract with reader: movement, hook, repetition

It is possible for teacher and student to employ the hook from a prewriting stage through later stages of organization. It is even useful as a final checking device. A student of mine wrote a paper that did not satisfy her. She came to me with it and said: "What's wrong with this? I thought the hooks in the title were pretty good and that the paper would be convincing." I suggested that she write hooks, title, and the paragraph topic or "lead" sentences on a page for discussion.

Title: Power to Both Parents
Hooks: *power, both parents*
Topic Sentences:

1. Introduction: Some type of organization is necessary for a family if it is to be successfully maintained.
2. Neither the husband nor the wife should be the dominant figure in the family.
3. Although both parents should be equally involved in making decisions for the family, it may not be necessary for both to earn equal amounts of income.
4. Both parents are responsible for the discipline of the children, and they should share this responsibility equally.
5. The children also have a responsibility to the family unit.
6. *Conclusion:* Organization is important if a family is to be smoothly run.

After inspecting this, the student saw her own problem immediately. Paragraph 5 was hooked to an idea outside her topic. So she cut the paragraph and inserted a different one.

The hook, as we have discussed it, is an all-purpose device that crosses rhetorical barriers and can help the writer in various ways. But once he is into the paper and writing furiously along—then what? How can he produce "movement of ideas" inside the paragraph and from paragraph to paragraph? One fact is pretty clear; he won't always be able to get the job done by use of the sanctified topic sentence, nailed securely on top of a group of statements. As Richard Braddock demonstrated in 1974, the topic sentence is not the organizing principle of many standard paragraphs.[2] Professional writers have long known this. Thirty years before Professor Braddock's scholarly discussion of the paragraph, the Canadian humorist Stephen Leacock—who wrote more than two dozen books and made a good living as a writer—remarked:

> In the old-fashioned books on rhetoric much was made of the formation of paragraphs. Indeed the Scottish writers, who loved severity, took the paragraph in custody under a set of rules called the Laws of the Paragraph. But little need be made of this now. In the printer's sense a paragraph is becoming not a break in the sense, but a break in the type. It is made as a

gardener trims a border with a hoe, knocking a little gap wherever it looks pretty. It is part of the new need for "make-up" that goes with our magazines and newspapers of today. Even our books share it . . . . [The paragraph] remains as a division of the sense—a pause in a story, an opening of an argument. But it is doubtful if we can with any advantage reduce this to law. A paragraph is in reality a consequence not a cause. You don't make a paragraph; you merely, as it were, run out of breath. Now no one would plan his breathing for his exercise; he takes his exercise and his breathing must take the consequence.[3]

What is a paragraph? It is, or can be:

A place where writer and reader take a breath
A way of breaking up the lines of type on the page, thus giving
    visual relief
A logical unit
A rhetorical unit
An esthetic form, like a piece of sculpture
A part of the rhythm of the essay

A great many paragraphs do not have a rigid or predictable structure. Experienced writers often plan their strategies for larger units than the paragraph. As Herbert Read remarked in *English Prose Style*, "It is nearer the truth to say that a writer seizes upon some particular aspect of his subject and holds that aspect in his mind until he has seen it in all profitable lights. This process may take two or it may take twenty paragraphs. . . ."[4]

Here is an example of a writer seizing upon some particular aspect of his subject. The subject is the confusion in spelling practices during the Middle Ages:

Transition relates to previous paragraph

1. Certainly some of the confusion [in Middle English spelling] is a confusion of dialects. Many Middle English scribes, like their Anglo-Saxon predecessors, had a sense of phonetic values in letters, and tried to spell a

Details word the way they pronounced it. But
many others seem to have spelled with
the greatest abandon. We constantly
see the same word spelled in two ways
in adjacent lines, and I recall once
having noticed one word spelled four
different ways in four consecutive
Climactic general lines. We may probably assume that
statement leading scribes sometimes copied what they
into following saw and sometimes rendered words
paragraphs into a rough phonetic equivalent of
their own dialects; clearly this diver-
sity accounts for some of the confusion,
but by no means for all of it.

Transition 2. Consider the following bit of evidence, which I blundered upon in a
manuscript in the Huntington Library
at San Marino, California. The work is
a long collection of rhymed sermons in
Anglo-Norman, written by one Robert
de Greatham. The scribe who copied
No topic sentence, as the manuscript finished a line which
such, but an implied ended in a form of *pêche* (sin). Whether
topic idea: Some or not this particular scribe had some
scribes were careless Freudian interest in sin, when he
copyists flicked his eyes back to the manuscript
he was copying from he hit upon another *pêche* which was the last word in
the seventh line previous. Accordingly,
he copied the same seven lines twice,
which was no wonder. No doubt Robert
de Greatham was a faithful servant of
his Lord, but he was a very dull poet,
Example and the lines say so little that the scribe
could be excused for not realizing that
he had read this before somewhere.
But now the curious fact. No two of
these lines agree. Here was the same
scribe, with the same copy, who copied
the same passage twice within a quar-

ter hour, and he does not produce one single line which is identical in both copies. Nor is he consistent in his own spelling of common words.

Question: A transitional "lead" for a paragraph

3. Was this man a bungler, or someone who scarcely knew how to write? No, for we know something about him. The manuscript is vellum, and accordingly worth money; no beginner would have been allowed to touch it. Furthermore, the manuscript is clearly the product of a professional scriptorum, that is, of a business establishment which produced manuscript copies commercially.

Details

A note on it tells what it sold for; it is written in a rapid, easy, careless hand, in the script of a man who wrote for a living and could keep it up all day. We can tell, for instance, when he started in the morning—his hand is fresh and vigorous—when he went to confection,

Italicized sentence answers the question in the paragraph's first sentence and thus helps to hold the paragraph together

and when he stopped for a few minutes' rest. *He was a professional, and this was a routine, professional job.* Everything about the manuscript attests to that. The obvious fact about the copying is this: the copyist felt no obligation to copy what was before him. He looked at a line, and wrote it as he pleased, changing the order of the words if he felt like it, even substituting a synonym now and then, and spelling and punctuating as the spirit moved him. People

Climax of three paragraphs—the point of the whole passage

in the Middle Ages were not much concerned about spelling.[5]

Paragraph 1 of Laird's passage starts off with what looks like a topic sentence (but is really a transition), followed by supporting details. The last sentence, which climaxes paragraph 1, is a generalization that leads into paragraph 2, which has no stated topic sentence. Paragraph 3 begins with a question-transition;

moves through several details; comes to rest for a moment in the middle of the paragraph in what appears to be a concluding remark; and then moves on to the climax of the whole passage. Laird has written three paragraphs, all of them leading up to the last sentence— *People in the Middle Ages were not much concerned about spelling.* In a sense, we have here a small composition with a single "topic sentence"—or thesis, if you prefer. The paragraphs are neatly organized and smoothly written, but Laird has not created them by routine or mechanical methods. He has developed a single idea about spelling in the Middle Ages, carefully fitting his paragraphs to this idea and to each other.

Laird is an artful and interesting writer. There is no duller subject on earth than spelling, and spelling in the Middle Ages is a subject of cosmic dullness. But so pleasantly does Laird drift into his topic, talking to the reader over his shoulder, and so attractively does he introduce his evidence, particularly the bit about the careless scribe who copied seven lines twice and didn't get a single one of them "identical in both copies," that one is charmed with stuff that ought to be as dry as dust.

In defining the term *paragraph*, Herbert Read called it "a device of punctuation . . . . Like the other marks of punctuation . . . it may be determined by logical, physical, or rhythmical needs."[6] The logical needs of the paragraph have been discussed with some completeness by our textbooks. A "topic idea" can be expressed in or near the beginning, middle, or end of a paragraph. It can be unexpressed or implied. Considered physically, a paragraph is a group of sentences placed on a page. Since readers dislike reading very long blocks of material, occasional paragraph breaks are necessary for breathing space. Rhythmically considered, a paragraph is a rhetorical creation whose length, shape, and emphases are determined by many things—among them the writer's purpose, his subject, and the nature of his reader.

All this may be true, but perhaps we still wonder about the "tricks of the trade." Unquestionably, the competent writer gets from here to there by one procedure or another. Let us look at some of these procedures.

One that is commonly used can be symbolized by this diagram, which we will call *the double signpost:*

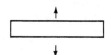

As Brandt remarked, an essay must move toward its conclusion. The writer has to pull the reader along behind him. One method of keeping the reader on the track is to leave a series of signposts that point two ways:

↑

"On a more profound level, this youthful impact at the box office . . . can lead to an appreciation of a film such as the current **Tell Them Willie Boy Is Here.**"[7]

↓

As the sentence and its diagram imply, the double signpost looks back. The writer has just been discussing "this youthful impact at the box office." And it looks forward, to a discussion of how one can appreciate a particular film "such as the current *Tell Them Willie Boy Is Here.*" From the same article, another double signpost:

↑

"So much for the survey of the change, its physical and financial appearance. To borrow from the title of one of Richard Lester's short subjects, *the American cinema and its audiences are now running, jumping, and standing still—all at the same time.*"[8]

↓

Here the writer gives us another sign of organization. *Backward*—he tells us he has surveyed a certain kind of change; *forward*—now he will consider the paradox of instability in American film and its audience. The double signpost is usually placed at the beginning of the paragraph. The first example used only one sentence to do its job; the second needed two. There is no rule implied here, except that signposts appear to be most efficiently employed in three or fewer sentences. If you use more than three, the reader may lose his way.

Writers of textbooks have not emphasized the double signpost. True, they often say a few words about "transitions," which they usually treat briefly by giving examples: *first, second, third, for instance, next, finally,* etc. These tend mainly to point forward. In their attempt to appear organized, inexperienced writers will often sprinkle their papers with such terms, hopefully leaving clues along the trail like dropped crusts of bread. We have all read the paper or article that desperately drops whole loaves and places them out in plain sight: *"My first point is . . . My second point is . . . Third and finally . . . ."*

The double signposts I quoted a paragraph back were taken from an ordinary piece of journalism published about ten years ago in the *Saturday Review*. But is the double signpost no more than an ordinary journalist's trick? I pick up a glossy work of scholarship and wisdom entitled *The Modern Researcher*, and find:

"The historical method, as the reader has already seen for himself, ascertains the truth by much the same means as are used for that purpose in daily life. The mental operations are those of common sense. But one must immediately add that common sense is not so common as its name suggests. . . ."

"Such improvisers would make poor historians. To be sure, even good scholars will at times take a holiday from method. . . ."

"For a good example, we may instance a book published in England a few years ago, . . ."

"Neither in this passage nor elsewhere in the book is any evidence presented except that of the well-known close companionship of brother and sister. . . ."

"Inexcusable it is, because the rule of "Give evidence" is not to be

violated with impunity. No matter how possible or plausible the author's conjecture. . . ."

↓

↑

"The particular error we have been examining is worth a word more. . . ."

↓

These authors—Jacques Barzun and Henry Graff—are academicians, but they are no less aware than our journalist from *Saturday Review* of the need to leave a trail for the reader to follow. Picking a passage at random from their book, I have simply quoted from the beginnings of six successive paragraphs.[9] Looking closely at these six signposts, one may note two things.

First, they may or may not be "topic sentences." Second, they offer a possibility to the reader that most writers of ordinary prose seldom consider. This is that if you are suddenly dropped into the middle of the trail Barzun and Graff have left for the reader, you have some idea—however small—of where you are. Excellent writers often appear to believe that their readers are like crazy parachutists, likely to swoop down and land with a thump at any old place in the argument. I again open Barzun and Graff at random:

↑

"To this intense moralism there was added in the Middle Ages a ready belief in the occurrence of the supernatural on earth."[10]

↓

Our parachutist picks himself up, peers around, and happily discovers—thanks to the authors' technique—that he is somewhere in the middle of moralism, the Middle Ages, and its belief in the supernatural. An untutored author, by contrast, would typically fail to use the opening prepositional phrase, and would put the rest of the sentence something like this: ". . . there was added at a particular time a strong spiritual belief which we must discuss at some length." If lucky, he might stumble onto his real topic four or five lines down. Inexperienced writers often have a dreadful time getting going—they habitually *begin* to *start* to *commence.*

Assuming that the double signpost is a genuine element in clear organization, how can we explain its neglect by theorists and textbook writers? The main reason, I suspect, is implied in F. L. Lucas' little story:

> Clarity, of course, has its limitations and its dangers. First, do not count on your readers to be grateful. I remember how, after taking a good deal of pains to make as lucid as possible a small manual on Tragedy, I had from a spy in Girton [England] a report of the verdict of one of its readers there: "Quite good, you know; but so simple!"[11]

Even more than the English, Americans are afraid of the simple and clear. Our unspoken premise is: if something can be easily understood, it must be essentially trivial. According to this premise, the first characteristic of the worthy argument is its ability to increase puzzlement. The best of all possible arguments would leave our parachutist in mist and fog and total darkness. I know a university teacher of composition who likes to declare: "I will fail students who start a paragraph with a question." He would then fail thousands of professional writers who use the question as an organizational device, as Charlton Laird did in his third paragraph on the medieval scribe.

You will recall my question at the beginning: how does one produce movement of ideas on the page? The answers so far may seem obvious, even trite. Worse, they are made after the fact. In other words, I have merely analyzed several pieces of writing, but have not shown how to *produce* organization from the muddle of ideas a writer has in his head but not on paper.

Of course there are familiar suggestions available: "Write an outline." But an outline tells you only how you plan to write a particular argument, not arguments in general. Besides, outlines don't always work; mine seldom do. I often outline a section after I write it, a practice which allows me to see where I went wrong. Axiom: if you don't know where you are going, at least find out where you have been. This procedure, although a little haphazard, gives the writer some control over his material.

The ancients, many of whom hated the haphazard in anything, were always telling us to lay arguments on a rhetorical bed of Procrustes. For example:

1. *Exordium*—makes the reader attentive and friendly to you; ready to listen to your argument.
2. *Narratio*—states the historical facts in the question or problem being argued; should be clear and brief. Terms may be defined here.
3. *Divisio*—lists the main points of your argument. Thesis stated.
4. *Confirmatio*—presents the main argument; gives your proofs and evidence of probable truth.
5. *Confutatio*—refutes any real or possible opposing arguments.
6. *Peroratio*—concludes.

In modern terms, this is hardly more than:

Introduction
Proof
Refutation
Conclusion

Other patterns and devices are possible—you will find them in modern textbooks, including mine—but I will spare you their rehearsal.

There is perhaps only one (fairly) sure technique for producing organization in arguments: make some kind of contract with the reader—and stick to it. By this I do not mean that you guarantee a certain kind or pattern of organization—analogic, enumerative, contrastive, and so on. Rather, you guarantee to tell the reader something, and then you tell it.

For an example of a "writer's contract," let us inspect parts of a chapter written by Moses Hadas. At the time he published this, Professor Hadas—who had been chairman of the Department of Greek and Latin at Columbia University—was Jay Professor of Greek there. The chapter begins (emphasis created by boldface is mine):

From his first hour of life, when he was laid at his father's feet for **ceremonial acceptance**, the Roman lived in **a world of order** and **ritual**. He was, above all else, a **traditionalist**, a man who acknowledged change only grudgingly, and in domestic and social life hardly at all. Thus, while Rome itself was changing from a small city-state into a vast empire, its people maintained **the old ceremonies** and **customs almost unaltered.**

I skip five paragraphs to Hadas' discussion of marriage:

1. Once the match had been made, the betrothal was formalized in a **ritual.** At this **ceremony** the dowry was stipulated, and the bride-to-be, usually 14 or 15, received gifts and a pledge of marriage from her fiancé. Symbolic of this pledge was a metal ring worn on the third finger of her hand, from which a nerve was believed to lead directly to the heart.

2. Of the three different forms of marriage in vogue at the time of the early Empire, the most **formal,** used only by patricians, was the *confarreatio.* Under this contract, the woman's person and property were surrendered to her husband. For women who demanded greater freedom from their husbands, there were other, less rigid forms of marriage. In the *coemptio,* the groom symbolically "bought" the bride from herself. In the *usus,* somewhat similar to modern common-law marriages, the couple would agree to live as man and wife without any religious ceremony. After a year they were considered legally married. In such an alliance the woman might actually retain rights to property she owned—provided she absented herself from her husband's bed and board for three nights every year.

3. **Weddings**—especially the *confarreatio* form—were **rich in ceremonial.** The date was selected with care: many days of the year, including all of March and May and half of June, were considered unlucky. On the eve of the big day, the bride dedicated her childhood dress and toys to the household gods of her father. On the day of her wedding she attired herself in a special tunic, fastened about her waist by a woolen girdle in a "Hercules knot," which only the groom might untie. Over this she wore a saffron cloak and a veil of flaming orange. Her hair was arranged in an elaborate six-plaited coiffure, topped by a crown of flowers.

4. The wedding was conducted by two priests. The couple sat side by side on stools covered with a single sheepskin, and

shared a sacred wheat cake and clasped hands as a sign of union while the marriage contract was read, witnessed and sealed.

5. Following an important wedding, the assembled guests feasted until nightfall. As the festivities ended they were offered pieces of a wedding cake made of meal steeped in new wine and then baked on bay leaves. Then the bridal party proceeded to the home of the bridegroom, accompanied by flutists and boys who chanted the *epithalamium*, a cheerful and often ribald song. Nuts, symbolizing fertility, were distributed to children along the way.[12]

Hadas begins his chapter by making a contract with the reader, a bargain implied by the terms **ceremonial acceptance, a world of order and ritual, traditionalist, the old ceremonies,** and **customs almost unaltered.** As he discusses the Roman marriage, he continues to fulfill the contract with terms like **formal, ceremony, ceremonial,** and **ritual.** As he implies in his introduction, **ritual** is a key word. Not only is it the major term in this writer's contract; it also helps to shape the material which follows—particularly the examples in paragraphs 3, 4, and 5. The point is important. Throughout their lives in school, from the early grades to the Ph.D., writers are taught to avoid repetition of words. As a long-time supervisor of composition teachers, I have seen hundreds of red *Repets.* in marginal comment on themes. And hundreds of undergraduates have told me their high school teachers considered repetition to be a sin second only to beginning a sentence with *but* or *and:* "You used this word two paragraphs back; find another one here."

Yet repetition—or repetitive "echoing" by use of loose synonyms—is a necessary technique of organization. The writer uses it to shape his material. He hacks his way through the underbrush of his own mind by continual reference to key terms or their echoes—**ritual, formal, ceremonial.** A trail thus blazed can be easily followed by readers no matter how cold it has become over the years. It should be a relief to both teachers and students to learn that the Jay Professor of Greek at Columbia is not afraid of repetition.

Hadas' contract is fulfilled in a second way, by a series of promising statements that point forward: "Weddings—especially the *confarreatio* form—were rich in ceremonial" (in paragraph 3). Here Hadas promises to discuss the ceremonies in the *confarreatio* form, and so he does for three paragraphs, two of which have no topic sentence as such. The paragraph breaks are partly a place to take a breath, partly a slight shifting of the subject. Here we can recall Herbert Read's metaphor: to see all the "profitable lights" of a subject, we hold it up, turning it this way and that, the facets of the subject reflecting now one idea, now another.

I have mainly ignored one important fact about the argument that Hadas successfully organized. It is that he makes the whole thing "move" by the use of fact, example, and detail. This technique we are all familiar with; and so, except for this mention, will ignore it.

Before finishing these comments on organization, one other small thing—actually, a reminder of an earlier remark. "The only way one can discuss movement in an essay or speech," said William Brandt, "is to look at specific examples."[13] This is a useful point to remember. We all know the *schemata* found in textbooks of the last two thousand years, and helpful they can be. Since they are the rhetorical artifacts of common sense, we will find traces of them in the most original and patulous of arguments. *Schemata* aside, however, the most compelling and useful notes on organization are written only after inspecting individual cases.

5 A View of Argument

*"A man who makes an assertion puts forward a claim—
a claim on our attention and to our belief."*
Stephen E. Toulmin, *The Uses of Argument*[1]

About thirty years ago, I was a young engineer working on a variety of commercial projects and experiments. I was having difficulty with the required writing—memos, letters, short daily reports, sometimes longer reports on finished work. After bogging down on one piece of writing, I went to the department head with my tale of woe.

"Well" he said, "try thinking this way. Imagine that every piece you write is an argument that asks a reader to *believe* or *do* something. Or both. Your job is to convince the reader to believe what you want him to, to do what you suggest. Lead him by the hand through your report or letter. When you think he might stumble, stop and find out why, and where you went wrong—because *you* are responsible for keeping him on his feet."

I went away feeling that my mind had been rinsed out with uncommon good sense. I had taken two full years of composition at the university, but no one (as I recall) had ever talked about argument except as a type of writing one took a course in. For example, there was the second-year sequence in composition: a quarter each of narration/description, exposition, and argumentation. Nor do I recall any discussion of the reader and his hardships.

For my professors, I guess he didn't exist. As for the possibility that he might "stumble"—the metaphor opened up a new way of thinking about the difficulties a reader could find as he followed me over the rhetorical hills peculiar to scientific work.

But, as it turned out, scientific rhetoric was not so peculiar as I thought. I now have students ranging in age from sixteen to sixty, and most of the papers they write are argumentative—they are trying to get people to believe or do something. And they are often frustrated by the seeming mismatch of their material and the form they want to pour it into. Ideas don't fit; ideas hang out; ideas they want to express won't go where they wish to put them.

I am, of course, very sympathetic. The same difficulties often overwhelm me, I tell them. And there are no easy answers. But there is a view of argument that may be of help. In this view, you try to isolate and solve these problems:

> What is your *stance*—who are you? Who is your reader? What is your point?
>
> Since you can't say everything on your topic, what things will you omit and why?
>
> When you have decided on the things you can say, you can't say them all at once. How will you arrange your ideas?
>
> Argument is a process of "revelation" (one reads from the top to the bottom of a page). How have you planned to make this process work?
>
> For full and convincing revelation, some ideas require more time and detail than others. How will you *pace* your argument?
>
> Where can the main point of your argument be most strategically placed?
>
> Argument is not solipsistic. It is a humane endeavor humanely performed. To be genuinely convincing, an argument ordinarily appeals to something outside you and your reader —a belief, an ethic, a body of evidence, a method of proof, a standard of behavior, etc. Such an appeal involves the *reality principle*. How will you use this principle?

The successful argument often seems to pick up a topic and examine it for the reader's benefit. Such an examination is partly a joint venture—rather as if reader and writer, standing side by side, were inspecting an exotic plant. "Look at this leaf; now consider the root structure . . . ." At the end of such an exercise in examining an argument, both reader and writer may be subtly and forever changed.

I will analyze a few contemporary nonfiction arguments in some detail, rather as a literary critic might analyze a play, novel, or poem. My questions, roughly speaking, are: What does the writer of an argument tend to do? Why does he do it? How and when is he successful? What can we learn from such analyses? Let's begin with a well-made argument published a few years ago.

Tango Crosses A Film Frontier[2]
by Joy Gould Boyum

1. Contrary to any rumors you may have heard, the price for Bernardo Bertolucci's *Last Tango in Paris* is just right—$5 a ticket, the going rate for pornographic films. For make no bones about it, *Last Tango in Paris* is pornography.

2. This is not to raise questions about Bertolucci's intentions. It's important to make this clear because every definition of pornography, from that in the American Heritage Dictionary to the one in the Penguin English Dictionary, speaks of it as *intended* to arouse sexual excitement or lascivious feelings. But intentions have always seemed a useless criterion. How ever do we measure them? "Never trust the teller, trust the tale," D. H. Lawrence wisely admonished us. Can we, then, draw "intentions" from the work, itself? It's particularly difficult to do so in pornography since its effects are so highly variable.

3. Nor do I mean to raise questions about *Last Tango in Paris'* "redeeming social value"—to quote the 1966 Supreme Court decision. Again, we can find our social redemption where we like and there are even those among us who will argue that searching for it in the individual merits of a pornographic work is beside the point. Pornography itself, they claim, serves a useful social value. Like prostitution, it drains off antisocial impulses.

4. Nor do I mean that *Last Tango in Paris* is not art. For although I suspect that pornography can rarely be good art and less often great art, *The Last Tango*, in both its visual texture and its acting, reflects not only great care and skill, but indeed

brilliance. Where it does not break through its form to overwhelm us with its content, it is absolutely beautiful to look at.

5. Still, its "beauty" or even its "truth" notwithstanding,
Last Tango in Paris is pornography, primarily because it conceives man totally in terms of his erotic being, because it
separates his sexual identity from his total identity, and makes
everything that it presents relative to the erotic sequences at its
core. It is not insignificant, in this context, that when at its end,
the film seems to attempt to pass judgment on its own viewpoint,
implying that man cannot live by sex alone after all, it becomes
startlingly melodramatic and strikingly unconvincing.

6. While its view of man as his genitals is sufficient to make
clear the film's *modus operandi*, it declares itself pornography
in several other ways as well. Its realm is fantasy, the classic
realm of all pornography; its sexual mode is obscenity, with
those familiar pornographic manifestations of aberation and
physical cruelty; its essential emotion is rage and as psycho-
analysts tell us, rage is precisely what pornography is all about.
Its characters are generalizations, who, moreover, fall into the
classic pornographic relationship of victim and victimizer,
with the inevitably female victim revelling in her role as object;
and finally, as in the works of our most famous pornographer
of all, the Marquis de Sade, *Last Tango in Paris* identifies sex
with death.

7. A 45-year-old American named Paul (Marlon Brando)
meets a 20-year-old girl named Jeanne (Maria Schneider) in an
empty apartment in Paris. Their meeting immediately takes us
into the realm of fantasy since neither has any reason at that
point to be searching for an apartment. But we hardly have
time to even notice their motives, for within five minutes of
their meeting and without bothering to either lie down or take
off their clothes, Paul and Jeanne are fornicating under the
camera's absolutely unblinking eye. The "For Rent" sign
naturally comes down, and the clothes shortly thereafter come
off (mostly Miss Schneider's since Mr. Brando, befitting his
being as a male and major movie star, discreetly keeps his
private parts from public view), as both agree to make of the
apartment a world of sex. Here they meet as nameless, pastless
creatures; he, to abuse her verbally, to brutalize her physically,
and ultimately, through the acts in which he engages her, to

annihilate her very femaleness; she, merely to experience ecstasy.

8. Although the film does not confine itself to the apartment or to the sexual encounters between Paul and Jeanne, it never relaxes its pornographic attitude. Following the girl outside the apartment, for example, it shows her less as an individual than it develops her role as victim, her world as imaginary, and her particular fantasies as infantile. Mostly, we see Jeanne with her fiancé (Jean-Pierre Leaud) who is—what else, since this is 1973?—a filmmaker and nothing very much else besides. The subject of his current film is the girl herself and he is constantly framing her, shooting her, recording her intimate reactions, and, so then, violating her. He is also, by asking her to exist for and in fantasy, contributing to her infantilism. "We can't live like this, like children," he says at one point, stepping out of what little character he has, "we're adults."

9. Following Paul, Bertolucci's film reveals that he is preparing for the funeral of the wife who has supported him for the past five years on the proceeds of a sleazy hotel and who for reasons unknown has committed suicide with a razor blade. The vagueness of her motives is important to Paul's generality as character. One-time boxer, one-time actor, one-time farm boy, middle-aged and miserable, both Paul and his pain remain sufficiently ill-defined to allow for the easy identification typical of pornography. Paul outside the apartment, then, is not developed very much beyond Paul inside. And when we see him with his wife's mother, with her lover, and with her corpse as well, the sequences serve no other end but that of revealing to us the sources and meaning of his sexually expressed outrage: death, which Paul in his despairing anger sees as the greatest obscenity of all. Death incites Paul to sex and sex ultimately leads Paul to death. He may, at the end, declare his love for Jeanne; but our options are confined to disbelief on the one hand, or on the other, belief in a love based on violent sexuality.

10. Because *Last Tango in Paris* is pornography and because it is pornography articulated with the emotional intensity special to Brando the actor and the visual intensity special to Bertolucci the director, it is difficult to imagine any viewer who would not be either intensely aroused or intensely disgusted. And because it is 1973, the era of pornography and lay analysis,

it is also difficult—except, that is, for the least self-conscious among us—to honestly admit to our feelings for or against the film. Whatever responses we have, after all, will ultimately say little about the art of *Last Tango in Paris* and a great deal about our own sexual orientation and sexual values—and finally, I suspect, a great deal about our values in general.

We read an argument from the top down. The writer customarily establishes his point (or points) by a series of revelations made "down the page." But only he can decide how they are to be presented. He is, as it were, uncovering an object which will eventually stand plain and unadorned before us. What will he decide to uncover first—a piece of logic, a small point of evidence, an important premise? Only one fact is certain: if there are things worth revealing, he can't—by the very nature of argumentation—reveal them all at once.

At the top of her argument (in paragraph 1), Boyum decides to make a major revelation which appears to be her main point: *"Last Tango in Paris* is pornography."

But in paragraph 2 she moves to another side of her argumentative object. This we may call a "negative issue," an idea that for some reason the writer may wish to set aside or ignore. The one she picks is the old one of *intention,* "a useless criterion," she remarks. In paragraph 3 she picks up a second negative issue, that of what the Supreme Court called in 1966 "redeeming social value." This, she believes, is also beside the point. In paragraph 4 she continues with her theme of negative issues, here removing from consideration the question of the film's art.

In paragraph 5, she reveals more of the thesis stated in the first paragraph. But now she creates a full predication, in both the logical and semantic senses, for her original point: The movie is pornographic because:

1. It conceives man totally in terms of his erotic being;
2. It separates his sexual identity from his total identity;
3. Everything that it presents [is] relative to the erotic sequences at its core.

Paragraph 6 does two jobs. It continues her attack on the movie as pornographic while adding to the definition of *pornography* as an act of deliberate creation. Boyum defines pornography as a set of characteristics: it is fantastic, obscene, aberrational, cruel, and full of rage. Its characters are not individualized people but "generalizations"—*the victim* and the *victimizer*. To cap her definition of pornography, the writer reminds us that like the Marquis de Sade, Bertolucci "identifies sex with death."

We might stop here for a moment to guess how as readers we would react to Boyum's argument if her editor has decided, perhaps for reasons of space, to cut her essay at the end of paragraph 6. Unquestionably, at this point, we have already learned a good deal. We know she believes that *Last Tango in Paris* belongs to a certain literary genre; that the so-called "intentional fallacy" is still alive in the minds of critics; that certain other issues—such as those of redeeming social value and the question of art—may be set aside in criticizing a work like this; that pornography has certain consistent characteristics.

Indeed, if an editor were to cut, he might well do so at the end of paragraph 6, where Boyum makes perhaps the most telling point so far—that the guiding theme of the movie is the same as the theme of de Sade's work: the identification of sex with death. And since de Sade is one of the most revolting men in history, will not the reader also easily accept *Last Tango In Paris* as one of the most revolting movies of our time?

Given these considerations, why did our writer continue? What is left for the argument to do that it hasn't already done?

Boyum apparently believed that she had not finished examining her topic; there are more revelations to be made. In paragraphs 7, 8, and 9 she now explains plot and character, giving us an idea of the action and how Bertolucci views his people. She also returns to the point of her argument with expressions like "realm of fantasy" (paragraph 7) and "it never relaxes its pornographic attitude" (paragraph 8). Throughout paragraphs 7-9, she continues to remind us that what the movie audience sees before it—all those ill-defined characters and actions—are typical of pornography.

There is an old rule in textbooks (and thousands of teachers have repeated it) which says: don't start a new argument in your conclusion. But our writer does so. After repeating her observation that the movie is pornographic, she leaps to an implication about one of the most important of value judgments. What does this movie—this cultural artifact—say about us as a people, about "our own sexual orientation and sexual values . . . about our values in general"? As readers we can infer that it says something rather unpleasant. According to Boyum, an important artist has encouraged us to believe in "the greatest obscenity of all"—not just rage and hatred, but sex-in-death. Moreover, unlike the great tragic artists of history, he has made this view of life not merely attractive but beautiful. And by this view of life, she says, we would of necessity be either "intensely aroused or intensely disgusted." Her argument is clearly about much more than mere pornography. In addition, we may note that this "much more" has been deliberately kept back. It is a final revelation, teasingly unrevealed until the last paragraph, even until the last sentence.

Let us set aside any final judgment of Boyum's success in this argument until after the next example. This new example is an argument on roughly the same topic, published within three months of the essay we have just read.

Brando's Role: A Boring Slob[3]
by Mike Royko

1. There's a scene in *Last Tango in Paris* when Brando talks to his young mattressmate about his unhappy boyhood on a farm.

He had a date, see, and he was all dressed up to take the girl to a basketball game.

But his father, a mean man, told him he had to milk the cow before he left.

So he milked the cow, and because of his father's callousness, he hurried off to his date with cow dung on his shoes.

"I was in a hurry, and I didn't have time to change my shoes," Brando tells the girl. "Later on, it smelled in the car. I can't remember very many good things [about his childhood]."

That is one of the scenes that has prompted some of the nation's best-known critics to rave about *Last Tango* as a great work of art.

2. But let's stop for just one moment and think about this scene.

There is a middle-aged man, talking about how, many years ago, his mean dad caused him to go on a date with cow dung on his shoes. It is pretty obvious that this experience led to his present condition of cynicism, withdrawal, toughness, sadness, and general indifference to his fellow man. And maybe also his manner with strange young ladies—which includes rape, sodomy, and sexual sadism and masochism.

I have to assume that the cow-dung incident is important, because it is one of the lengthiest speaking parts of the film.

Now, if you were sitting in a tavern and some guy started telling you about how he once was humiliated because he went on a date with cow dung on his shoes, what would you say?

Of course, you would ask: Why didn't you wipe them off, dummy?

How long does it take to wipe off a pair of shoes with a damp cloth? Ten seconds or twenty? In a minute or two you can even give yourself a pretty good shine.

3. Once you asked that question, the bore in the tavern would probably shut up, which is what somebody should do if he doesn't have sense to wipe cow dung off his shoes.

But here we have a two-hour movie all about just that kind of jerk, and the critics say it is wonderful.

I had gone to a private screening of *Tango* for newsmen expecting to be slightly startled by the now famous sex scenes, but I figured it was worth it to see the rest of the highly acclaimed movie.

As it turned out, the sex scenes—and there aren't many— were the only parts of the film that kept me from dozing off. Take them away, and it is as boring a movie as has ever been made.

Nelson Algren, the great writer, summed it up when the screening ended.

"Why, he's just a slob," Algren said about the Brando character.

4. That's about it. It is a two-hour movie about a self-pitying, self-centered, whining, foul-mouthed, boring slob.

And his girl friend has to be the dumbest broad ever put on the screen—a sort of My Friend Irma with her pants off. What can you say about a young lady from a fine family who takes up with the first seedy, middle-aged creep who rapes her?

I don't necessarily object to slobs, or movies about slobs, just so long as they are fascinating slobs, colorful slobs, adventurous slobs, or champion slobs. Henry VIII, for instance, got more and more interesting as his slobbiness increased.

But Brando plays a boring slob. You'll find one or two in every barracks, in every bar, or standing in front of a judge in a police court.

If you'll let him, he'll talk for two hours about why he can't stop drinking, or why he can't live with his wife, or why he can't hold a job. And, when he finishes explaining, he will start right over again.

5. So what you do is defend yourself by throwing in a word or two of your own: So, it's your liver, drink; or, so quit moaning and divorce her; or, you don't want to work, then be a bum, just pay for your own drinks.

But unless you are a masochist, you don't sit there listening for two hours.

That's what you'll be doing, though, if you put down the $4 or $5 it will cost to see this dud.

The puzzle is why so many critics think it is an outstanding movie, a remarkable breakthrough in cinema art, a film milestone, blah, blah.

I have a theory. Not only about this movie, but about movie critics in general.

Many of them have spent so much of their young lives sitting and watching movies that they haven't been exposed to enough reality.

Movie critics often are people who have been film fanatics since childhood. When their pals were hanging around alleys or getting into fights, they were at a movie. When everybody else in the barracks went to town and got falling-down drunk, they went to a movie.

And when they got jobs on newspapers, instead of looking at dead bodies in the morgue, human tragedy in police stations and courts, and skulduggery in the political arenas, they were reviewing dead bodies, tragedy and skulduggery as presented on a movie screen.

6. Take Pauline Kael, the most influential critic, whose praise touched off the fame of *Tango*. I don't suppose many of her neighbors have been drunken wife-beaters, or that she has spent many days listening to the self-destructive wine-heads from Wilson Ave. or Clark St. tell a judge how they got into their mess.

If she had, she would have looked up at Brando and said: "I

know him, that's my dog-kicking neighbor Charlie. His wife
put him under a $2,000 peace bond."

Miss Kael simply hasn't spent enough time with slobs, that is
clear. If she thinks Brando and his dung-covered shoes are so
great, she would have had to give five stars to Slats Grobnik's
runny nose.

At first glance, Royko's organization is that of the typical
newspaper column—short, choppy paragraphs that tend to group
themselves around a subject rather than develop it. But his
argument does have a definite development, and does reveal itself in
certain steps. Royko's strategy is both planned and precise, taking
six units to complete its revelations.

In unit 1, we have the dung scene explained, a scene (Royko
remarks) "that has prompted some of the nation's best-known
critics to rave about *Last Tango* as a great work of art." Unit 2 drops
us into a tavern, which is meant to represent real life. In real life,
you can wipe dung off your shoes and go on about your business.

Unit 3 gives us an apparent thesis: the film is dull, "as boring a
movie as has ever been made." It is a movie about slobs; even "the
great writer" Nelson Algren says so. Unit 4 repeats and expands
upon the thesis. Here Royko deals with what I called earlier a
"negative issue." He does not object to slobs as such, not to
"fascinating slobs, colorful slobs, adventurous slobs." But he objects
to Brando for the same reason that he would object to a boring slob
in an army barracks, a bar, or a police court.

Now unlike Boyum, Royko is partly at war with his reader.
Most satirists are. (I won't stop to comment on the complexities of
satire as an art form; it is so rich and varied that any convincing
discussion of the topic would take a book to complete.) One element
in Royko's technique is to set up the reader to expect one thing—here
comes the satirist's feint, but look out for the right cross to the jaw a
second later—and get another. This argument seems to be about
Brando and *Last Tango In Paris*. And so it is. But it is more about
the sort of people (in particular, certain influential movie critics)
who call bad works of art good. The real point of Royko's piece—its
artistic and argumentative center—lies in the middle of unit 5:
"Many [of the critics] have spent so much of their young lives sitting
and watching movies that they haven't been exposed to enough
reality."

The remainder of the argument develops this point, to which Royko has been leading all along. Again his technique is to drop us into real life: alleys, barracks, courts, and police stations. The influential critic Pauline Kael, says Royko, probably does not know about the real life of drunken wife-beaters, self-destructive wine-heads, or a dog-kicking neighbor named Charlie.

It is easy to look at Royko's column as merely a piece of satiric journalism. The typical tricks of the satirist are here, ranging from alliterative terms of diminishment like "mattressmate" to ironic incongruity created by juxtaposition:

> ... his mean dad caused him to go on a date with cow dung on his shoes. It is pretty obvious that this experience led to his present condition of cynicism, withdrawal, toughness, sadness and general indifference to his fellow man. And maybe also his manner with strange young ladies—which includes rape, sodomy, and sexual sadism and masochism.

But the satire, while necessary to the argument, is secondary. Royko has more in mind than just making an actor, a critic, and a movie look stupid. Primarily, he wants us to believe that an important element in our literary culture is untrustworthy. Many movie critics, he says, can't be trusted because they have had so little experience of the world that they don't know reality when they see it, not in bar and barrack—not, in fact, anywhere:

> And when they got jobs on newspapers, instead of looking at dead bodies in the morgue, human tragedy in police stations and courts, and skulduggery in the political arenas, they were reviewing dead bodies, tragedy and skulduggery as presented on a movie screen.

Let us pause here for some conclusions and judgments. On roughly the same topic we have looked at two different arguments. They differ in stance. Clearly, the writers have adopted different roles; they make different points; they do not think of their readers in the same way. Boyum's argument is relatively straightforward; it might in fact serve as the "second affirmative" speech in the standard format of contest debate. Royko's piece is satire, tending even to burlesque. It is useful to recall that *burlesque* goes back to *burla* ("ridicule"); and Royko diminishes his enemy through the time-honored device of making him look ridiculous.

The styles are also different. Boyum is smooth, serious, even-toned—her style has all the marks of good manners and a good education. Royko is (in the sample given here) a street urchin who has a way with words. He is a shot-and-a-beer man who does not mind sticking his thumb in the eye of his betters. He can use the big words, but one senses in this piece that he is more comfortable with expressions like *slob* and *seedy, middle-aged creep*.

But let us not make too much of the obvious differences in the stance and style of these arguments. Boyum wrote for the educated reader of *The Wall Street Journal;* Royko for the possibly less educated reader of the *Chicago Daily News*. But the *News* was the most literate paper in the Chicago of its time, and not a few of its writers—the columnist Sydney Harris, for example—employed a stance and style very similar to Boyum's. For that matter, Mike Royko could adopt what might be called the American Standard Style whenever he chose. His best-selling book *Boss*, written on the career of Chicago's Mayor Daley, is an example.

We should be more interested in the similarities between these arguments than in their differences. Both follow an argumentative structure of "revelation." They hold up an object for discussion before the reader. They take hold of the object by a particular handle. Then they start to reveal the various aspects, characteristics, qualities, and good and bad points of that object. Every revelation is done for the sake of the argument *in relation to* the reader—to how he may react. A negative reaction at the wrong time is a serious mistake in argument.

"Negative issues" are a case in point. The successful argument anticipates the reader's curiosity, misunderstanding, or objection. Early on, Boyum gets three such issues out of the way: they are revealed and set aside. Similarly, Royko anticipates an objection that he might be prejudiced against slobs as such—"I don't necessarily object to slobs . . . ." It is curious that in American society the feeling against snobbery is so pervasive that Royko apparently believes he must defend himself against a possible charge of anti-slob snobbery—in a piece which itself employs some of the rhetoric of the literate American slob.

Both writers believe that they must make their theses and major points very clear. Within the limits of the space allotted they are as clear and exact as it is possible to be. We know what the writers intend to convince their reader of—at each proper stage of revelation. This technique is of great importance. The arguer has to carry his reader along, balancing always certain delicate difficulties. Will the reader stay interested? Will he accept the implied stance of the argument? Will he accept each stage in the revelations? Will he agree that any "negative issues" really should be put aside— or will he stop and insist that one or more of them should be picked up and dealt with right there? The problem of *pacing* is vital in successful argumentation. You can't go too fast or too slow; too much explanation is as bad as too little.

Beyond these matters, both writers are similar in that they employ what might be called a *super-thesis*. In the process of revelation, a writer has to give his reader a reasonably clear sense of where the argument is going. Thus we get what textbooks call the *deductive* pattern of organization, which implies a sense of early direction in the argument. Boyum uses the simple thesis-like statement in her first paragraph: *"Last Tango in Paris* is pornography." Royko employs the burlesque contrast in the first two units of his argument, and these are followed by his thesis-like statement in unit 3: without the sex scenes, "it is as boring a movie as has ever been made."

Yet toward the end of each argument, both writers reveal a more important idea, one which they have been leading up to and wish to leave resonating in the reader's mind—a *super-thesis*. For Boyum, it is the idea that our culture is defective; there is something wrong with a value system that allows a work like *Last Tango in Paris* to exist. For Royko, it is a fairly similar but more limited idea. There is something wrong with a group of us—the movie critics. Their value system is defective because they cannot tell celluloid horrors from real ones. In a sense, both super-theses are classic in that they point to human defects that are related to defects in a society. But neither writer proposes a solution. They shout *Fire!* but drag no fire hoses to the blazing building.

Do these two arguments succeed? Let us withhold judgment until one final point is made about argumentation. Much of what I have said about the two arguments under discussion has at least some validity. This is a way of saying that certain points of my own are without doubt badly put, ambiguously expressed, or just plain debatable. I do believe, though, that one cardinal principle of argument is less debatable than the others. It is more important than the others. And upon it—more than the others—might well be based any judgment about the value of a particular argument.

This can be called the *reality principle*. If other matters are more or less equal, the success of an argument may depend on how well a writer has got outside the prison of his own mind in order to observe and report upon what he finds in the real world. With George Orwell, we can believe that the things of the world—from trees to human skin to Beethoven's *Ninth*—are really there. This was the great theme of Orwell's work on the relationship of language to politics. In the shadow world of *Nineteen Eighty-Four*, for example, one could not say with reasonable certainty: *So-and-so exists*, or *That symphony was written in 1826*; or *My building is made of bad concrete and that is why it is falling down*.

In *Nineteen Eighty-Four*, the present and past were being recreated daily. One did not know that there was an 1826, and one was not allowed to say that the concrete is bad. To the totalitarian of *Nineteen Eighty-Four*, "Reality is inside the skull"—these are the word of O'Brien, the Party philosopher and torturer. Two and two are not necessarily four. "Sometimes," says O'Brien, "they are five. Sometimes they are three. Sometimes they are all of them at once."[4]

The *reality principle* says: *Reality is primarily outside the skull; and we can—if imperfectly and spasmodically—grasp pieces of it.* Argument is (in one sense) the art of interpreting such pieces of reality to ourselves and to others. That we always fail to some extent should not deter us.

Casting aside certain questions of taste (Royko's style may be irritating to some readers, for example), we can conclude that both of the arguments we have inspected succeed reasonably well. That they are quite different in some ways does not seem important. They both respect the reader's intelligence and his desire for order, form, and clarity. Above all, perhaps, they seem to respect our ability to judge certain realities. The act of sodomy, for example, is a fact outside ourselves. A man who is a bore is a "judgmentalized fact" perhaps—but he is *there* nonetheless, as surely as a piece of cow dung. There are those who mind neither cow dung nor bores, who burn the one and marry the other; but a question of taste is like a nervous cat: pick it up at your own risk. It is interesting that Joy Gould Boyum found it "difficult to imagine any viewer [of *Last Tango*] who would not be either intensely aroused or intensely disgusted." Mike Royko, it would seem, was only intensely bored.

There are nine and ninety ways of making an argument, and many of them—given the proper circumstances—can succeed. Let us look at what would appear to be a very different one from those we have just seen.

The situation is fictional, but the argument is serious and can be treated as an exercise in genuine rhetoric. When Lon Fuller wrote it, he was Carter Professor of General Jurisprudence, Harvard Law School. In the *Postscript* to the piece, published in the *Harvard Law Review* in 1949, Fuller remarked:

> The case was constructed for the sole purpose of bringing into a common focus certain divergent philosophies of law and government. These philosophies presented men with live questions of choice in the days of Plato and Aristotle. Perhaps they will continue to do so when our era has had its say about them. If there is any element of prediction in the case, it does not go beyond a suggestion that the questions involved are among the permanent problems of the human race.[5]

The argument you are about to read is classic in both content and form. It is designed to tell us something about the law, about justice and human beings, and about the nature of argument itself.

Here is the background of the case. In May of the year 4299, five "cavers" entered a cavern to explore it. They were trapped in the cave by a huge landslide, and all efforts to rescue them failed. Ten men were killed by fresh landslides in a rescue effort. On the twentieth day of their imprisonment, communicating by radio to their rescuers outside, the cavers asked if they could survive for ten more days—by which time rescue seemed possible—if they ate a human being. (A physician had told them over the radio that they would probably die from starvation before the next ten days were up.) The cavers' question was answered in the affirmative. At this time, the radio went dead.

When the cavers were finally rescued, four of them were alive. They had killed and eaten one of their number, Roger Whetmore. Whetmore's fate had been decided by casting dice—a procedure agreed to by all the men involved. After their rescue, the surviving men were indicted for murder.

According to the legal practice of the time, several opinions were handed down on the case. The Chief Justice of the court stated that in his opinion the men were guilty of murder according to the law but that "some form of clemency" should be extended to the defendants. Another member of the court (Justice Foster) disagreed, and we pick up his argument here:[6]

1. I am shocked that the Chief Justice, in an effort to escape the embarrassments of this tragic case, should have adopted, and should have proposed to his colleagues, an expedient at once so sordid and so obvious. I believe something more is on trial in this case than the fate of these unfortunate explorers; that is the law of our Commonwealth. If this Court declares that under our law these men have committed a crime, then our law is itself convicted in the tribunal of common sense, no matter what happens to the individuals involved in this petition of error. For us to assert that the law we uphold and expound compels us to a conclusion we are ashamed of, and from which we can only escape by appealing to a dispensation resting within the personal whim of the Executive, seems to me to amount to an admission that the law of this Commonwealth no longer pretends to incorporate justice.

2. For myself, I do not believe that our law compels the monstrous conclusion that these men are murderers. I believe, on the contrary, that it declares them to be innocent of any crime. . . .

3. I take the view that the enacted or positive law of this Commonwealth, including all of its statutes and precedents, is inapplicable to this case, and that the case is governed instead by what ancient writers in Europe and America called "the law of nature."

4. This conclusion rests on the proposition that our positive law is predicated on the possibility of men's coexistence in society. When a situation arises in which the coexistence of men becomes impossible, then a condition that underlies all of our precedents and statutes has ceased to exist. When that condition disappears, then it is my opinion that the force of our positive law disappears with it. We are not accustomed to applying the maxim *cessante ratione legis, cessat et ipsa lex* to the whole of our enacted law, but I believe that this is a case where the maxim should be so applied.

5. The proposition that all positive law is based on the possibility of men's coexistence has a strange sound, not because

the truth it contains is strange, but simply because it is a truth so obvious and pervasive that we seldom have occasion to give words to it. Like the air we breathe, it so pervades our environment that we forget that it exists until we are suddenly deprived of it. Whatever particular objects may be sought by the various branches of our law, it is apparent on reflection that all of them are directed toward facilitating and improving men's coexistence and regulating with fairness and equity the relations of their life in common. When the assumption that men may live together loses its truth, as it obviously did in this extraordinary situation where life only became possible by the taking of life, then the basic premises underlying our whole legal order have lost their meaning and force.

6. Had the tragic events of this case taken place a mile beyond the territorial limits of our Commonwealth, no one would pretend that our law was applicable to them. We recognize that jurisdiction rests on a territorial basis. The grounds of this principle are by no means obvious and are seldom examined. I take it that this principle is supported by an assumption that it is feasible to impose a single legal order upon a group of men only if they live together within the confines of a given area of the earth's surface. The premise that men shall coexist in a group underlies, then, the territorial principle, as it does all of law. Now I contend that a case may be removed morally from the force of a legal order, as well as geographically. If we look to the purposes of law and government, and to the premises underlying our positive law, these men when they made their fateful decision were as remote from our legal order as if they had been a thousand miles beyond our boundaries. Even in a physical sense, their underground prison was separated from our courts and writ-servers by a solid curtain of rock that could be removed only after the most extraordinary expenditures of time and effort.

7. I conclude, therefore, that at the time Roger Whetmore's life was ended by these defendants, they were, to use the quaint language of nineteenth-century writers, not in a "state of civil society" but in a "state of nature." This has the consequence that the law applicable to them is not the enacted and established law of this Commonwealth, but the law derived from those principles that were appropriate to their condition. I have no

hesitancy in saying that under those principles they were guiltless of any crime. . . .

Foster's first step, in paragraph 1, is to shift the ground of the
argument. If the law says that the cavers have committed a crime,
then the law itself is suspect, convicted in "the tribunal of common
sense." The final question is one of justice, which may not be based
on the "personal whim" of those who dispense it.

In paragraph 2, Justice Foster states what appears to be his
thesis: the law "declares [the defendants] to be innocent of any
crime." He bases his opinion (paragraph 3) on the ground that the
law is inapplicable because the case is not governed by the law of the
Commonwealth at all but by what has been called "the law of
nature."

In paragraphs 4 and 5, Justice Foster develops this line of
reasoning by pointing out that laws themselves are based on the
reality of men's "coexistence in society": the term *coexistence* is used
four times in these paragraphs. The logic thus created by Foster
moves the argument toward a certain conclusion, toward which he
continues to progress in paragraph 6. He uses analogy: the cavers
were outside of legal jurisdiction in the cave as surely as they would
be outside of such jurisdiction a thousand miles beyond the borders
of the Commonwealth. Premise: "We recognize that jurisdiction
rests on a territorial basis." This is followed by another premise:
"Now I contend that a case may be removed morally from the force
of a legal order, as well as geographically." Therefore: both
physically and morally, the cavers were outside the law's jurisdiction.

Conclusion (paragraph 7): since the defendants were "not in a
'state of civil society' but in a 'state of nature,'... they were guiltless
of any crime."

In discussing an argument like Justice Foster's, it is tempting
to fall back on logical analysis and to maintain that it is an argument
based on textbook logic. After all, is not the law logical? Moreover,
anyone familiar with the standard textbook information on induction and deduction—with all the paraphernalia of Venn diagrams
and arguments reduced to syllogisms laid out in geometric neatness
on the page—is doubly tempted to use the logician's skills on
Foster's argument.

But harsh experience leads me to ignore the lure of textbook logical analysis here. First, such logic tends to be artificial. In truth, induction and deduction are no more than imperfect and inconsistent *strategies* of thinking which in real arguments are mainly used inconsistently and imperfectly. Man is not a machine, and he does not think like one. Furthermore, induction and deduction are interlocking strategies. In many important arguments, it is next to impossible to determine where one leaves off and the other begins.

We will learn more if we put aside the mechanical aspects of textbook logic and look—as we have before—at what the writer is really doing in his argument.

First, Justice Foster is aware (as any lawyer in his position must be) of stance. The pride of the jurist in his skills fairly glows on the page. A celebrated case can bring forth an equally celebrated opinion, quotations from which may ring down the halls of colleges of law. In his opening paragraph, Justice Foster acknowledges a legal enterprise of great pith and moment: the world is listening as the Court decides this difficult case.

But the world—like any other audience—will have to wait for this argument to unfold and for revelations to appear. The super-thesis comes first: if a Court like this says that these men are guilty, "then our law itself is convicted . . . ." What can he mean? wonders the reader. Answers are forthcoming. Paragraphs 2 and 3 associate the defendants' innocence with the idea of the "law of nature." This idea prepares the way.

Now comes the hinge of the argument. Any possible success of Justice Foster's larger conclusion turns upon the success of the small argument explained and defined in paragraphs 4, 5, and 6— that the law is predicated upon *coexistence in society*. In these spacious paragraphs, Foster turns the notion of coexistence over and around for his reader. He is deliberate, slow-paced, detailed. As I remarked earlier, he uses the word *coexistence* four times, and tolls the bell a fifth time in paragraph 6 ("men shall *coexist* in a group").

Having spent two-thirds of his argument on the issue of coexistence, Justice Foster concludes quickly: "I have no hesitancy . . . they were guiltless of any crime."

How does this argument differ from those by Joy Gould Boyum and Mike Royko?

First, and most obviously, it is a genre argument in that it is legal philosophy applied to a specific case. It is more self-consciously and explicitly analytical. Premises hang out as obviously as flapping sheets on a clothesline. A certain musty and conventional legal passion arises from it: "I am shocked . . . this tragic case . . . no longer pretends to incorporate justice."

Another difference is that the thesis of the piece is split between the top and bottom of the argument. These men are "innocent of any crime" (paragraph 2) because they were "not in a 'state of civil society' but in a 'state of nature'" (paragraph 7). Split theses are not unusual, particularly in arguments which require tight linkages between, and explanations of, important premises.

But perhaps we should be more impressed with the similarities among the three arguments. We have already noted that all three writers take deeply into account the question of stance and the necessity of careful (and carefully paced) revelation of major points. The reader will be served; he must be satisfied. Once he is so, stop. Don't maunder on. We recall the old adage in vaudeville: when your act is over, get off stage fast.

All three arguments employ the negative issue. For Justice Foster it is the argument of the Chief Justice that the cavers are murderers; the issue permeates Foster's analysis of the case. Note, for example, his reference in paragraph 1 to "a conclusion we are ashamed of . . . ."

And, finally, all three arguments employ the reality principle. Foster's work shows a deep sense of a real world existing outside and independent of majestic courts of law. Our law, he fears, will be "itself convicted in the tribunal of common sense . . . the enacted or positive law of this Commonwealth, including all of its statutes and precedents, is inapplicable to this case . . . ." Our "positive law," he remarks, is based upon the actual "condition" of man. Law serves man, not the other way around. In fact, Justice Foster's conclusion that the men are innocent is based upon his inspection of the real-world nature of the situation: "the law applicable to them" must be "derived from those principles that were appropriate to their condition."

Arguments like those we have analyzed are not unusual in American society. Indeed they are so commonplace in everyday American life that we tend to overlook them and the way they work.

When I act as consultant to business firms which are having trouble with their communications, my first step is to point out the obvious: "Ninety percent of what your people write—from computer manuals to letters answering complaints from customers—

are arguments. Recognize the fact, and you will begin to succeed in your writing. Ignore it, and you will lose a ton of money in numerous misunderstandings."

Let me supply a homely example. A part of my job a few years ago as Director of Rhetoric in a large university was to save money, time, and effort. A situation arose with a student (I'll call her Ms. Smith) which was costing everybody money, time, and effort—not to mention a good deal of irritation. Ms. Smith went to the Dean of her College in the university, claiming that one of my instructors had treated her "unfairly" in the freshman composition course. This Dean, a powerful and rather choleric gentleman, demanded that I produce the student's papers so that he could judge whether she had been treated "unfairly." I had to placate the Dean, but at the same time not anger my instructor, a hardworking and ethical woman who had bent over backwards to be fair to the student. Also, for political reasons I could not allow the Dean of another College, with no rights in my own College or Department, to pass judgments on the student's work. If I did so, my Department would consider me too stupid to continue in my job and would assign it to another and more artful professorial politician.

I wrote to the Dean the following argument:

To: Dean Blank
From: Director, Rhetoric
Subject: Susan Smith's final grade in Rhetoric 109

1. I have been out of town for a short time and have not been able to answer your letter of March 6 until now.

2. I have discussed the issues raised in your letter with the acting Department head, Professor _____, and with an associate dean in my College. I wish to report the following:

a. At the request (January 18) of Ms. Smith's father, I did a complete investigation of her work in Rhetoric 109. I wrote a detailed account (dated January 20) of her problems to her father, along with a copy of some of the instructor's comments. A part of the father's response (dated February 10) reads as follows: "The instructor's comments on her themes and your own statement on Susan's work indicate to me that Susan was to blame for her weak performance in the course." He accepted completely the explanation I gave him of his daughter's difficulties with the course.

b. The above-mentioned difficulties included a term paper

which was, as I told Ms. Smith, "technically speaking, a series of plagiarisms." If the instructor had wished, she could have sent Ms. Smith to the College for discipline for plagiarism.

c. I interviewed the instructor about Ms. Smith after her father wrote me. (By January 30, Ms. Smith had not seen either me or the instructor about her grade in the course.) She came to me for the first time on the fifteenth of February. I asked her to write an explanation of her complaint to me. I have this statement in her handwriting. She makes no reference in the statement to being treated "unfairly," the term you use in your letter to me.

d. At her request, I again went over her record of work in the course. I interviewed her instructor again to make sure that there were no difficulties I had missed the first time. On February 20, I wrote Ms. Smith that my second judgment about her work was the same as the first.

3. My conclusion is: the instructor has followed the policies laid down by the university and the English Department in regard to the evaluation of a student's work. All methods of review available have been employed in this matter, and the case is now closed.

The thesis of this practical argument is that the instructor is innocent of the student's charge. But just as important is an unstated super-thesis: the Rhetoric Division is conducting its business properly, and you [the Dean] were mistaken to get involved in it. I dealt with a mass of negative issues by ignoring them. I could have dwelt on the Dean's dismayingly weak grasp of professional ethics—one does not cross College lines in this way. His equally weak grasp of the facts of the case might have also been mentioned. I could have shown in some detail that the student was not to be trusted. I could have explained the methods of "review," but they were spelled out in printed sources easily available. I deliberately ignored these negative issues in order to let the Dean infer them in any way he might.

The argument proceeds, as most do, by a series of revelations. Paragraph 1 is obvious. Paragraph 2 says indirectly that I had marshalled my authorities and support. Paragraphs 2a and 2b give the facts of the case, including the reaction of the father, which the Dean did not know of. Paragraph 2c undermines Ms. Smith, who had been telling different stories to different administrators. Paragraph 2d gives more facts of the case and helps establish the Rhetoric Division's credibility. Paragraph 3 continues this theme; the revelations completed, it states a conclusion quickly: the case has been taken care of.

You will observe that, as with the arguments previously discussed, the writer is deeply concerned with the reality principle. In effect, this letter says to the Dean: "Outside of your brain and mine, certain events occurred. Here is what they are and how they are documented. These events are unarguable. Do they not lead to certain conclusions?" Furthermore, we might observe that the materials presented (revealed) in the letter are paced so that the reader is worked upon to maximum effect. Paragraph 1 is deliberately made brief and abrupt so that we can get quickly into the body of the letter. The pacing slows in paragraphs 2a through 2d so that the factual material can be absorbed. But it picks up again in the last short paragraph. "Get off stage fast."

To anticipate an objection: compared to the other arguments, the one just presented is too trivial; the rhetorical situation is not worth such extended discussion. Well, as Sam Johnson remarked, "There is nothing too little for so little a creature as man."

More to the point, perhaps, it is worth commenting that the great majority of written arguments are no more dignified or important than my letter to the Dean. The world's business is mainly trivial, but it is no trivial matter to get it done efficiently and inexpensively. Situations like the one Ms. Smith created have been known to tie up professors, administrators, appeal committees, and even college lawyers for weeks and months. All this is expensive and inefficient. The letter apparently worked; the rest was silence.

So far we have been inspecting arguments that have had some measure of success. Now to look at one that shows a certain degree of failure. As a typical reader might, let us interrupt to comment on passages when moved to do so.

What Christians Believe[7]
by C. S. Lewis

1. I have been asked to tell you what Christians believe, and I am going to begin by telling you one thing that Christians

don't need to believe. If you are a Christian you don't have to believe that all the other religions are simply wrong all through. If you are an atheist you do have to believe that the main point in all the religions of the whole world is simply one huge mistake. If you are a Christian, you are free to think that all these religions, even the queerest ones, contain at least some hint of the truth. When I was an atheist I had to try to persuade myself that the whole human race were pretty good fools until about one hundred years ago; when I became a Christian I was able to take a more liberal view.

From the beginning this has been a bit too simple. In particular, the opposition of believer/atheist strikes one as over-simple and unrealistic. A good many atheists do not believe—and do not *have* to believe—"that the main point in all the religions of the whole world is simply one huge mistake." An atheist may say: "*You* can believe, and *I* may understand your faith; but I myself cannot believe."

But, of course, being a Christian does mean thinking that where Christianity differs from other religions, Christianity is right and they are wrong. Like in arithmetic—there's only one right answer to a sum, and all other answers are wrong: but some of the wrong answers are much nearer being right than others.

Can we accept the analogy? He seems to be comparing apples and oranges.

2. The first big division of humanity is into the majority, who believe in some kind of God or gods, and the minority who don't. On this point, Christianity lines up with the majority—lines up with ancient Greeks and Romans, modern savages, Stoics, Platonists, Hindoos, Mohammedans, etc., against the modern Western European materialists. There are all sorts of different reasons for believing in God, and here I'll mention only one. It is this. Supposing there was no intelligence behind the universe, no creative mind. In that case nobody designed my brain for the purpose of thinking. It is merely that when the atoms inside my skull happen for physical or chemical reasons to arrange themselves in a certain way, this gives me, as a by-product, the sensation I call thought. But if so, how can I trust my own think-

ing to be true? It's like upsetting a milk-jug and hoping that the way the splash arranges itself will give you a map of London. But if I can't trust my own thinking, of course I can't trust the arguments leading to atheism, and therefore have no reason to be an atheist, or anything else. Unless I believe in God, I can't believe in thought: so I can never use thought to disbelieve in God.

More problems. And more serious ones. They start with the question, "How can I trust my own thinking to be true?" This is where a first objection to the passage involuntarily presents itself. But the real problem comes earlier with the premise that someone had to *design* a man's brain "for the purpose of thinking." Where in man's experience is the evidence for this extraordinary assertion?
The reader senses that Lewis is aware of a weakness here because, first, he slides so quickly, almost greasily, into the conclusion that he can't trust his own thinking unless there is "intelligence behind the universe." And, second, while his reader is trying to test the strength of the argument at this point, Lewis distracts him with the foolish analogy about the splash of the milk making a map of London.
The trouble with the conclusion at the end of the passage is that it must follow from the question-begging premise that there is "intelligence behind the universe." Not having proved this premise, Lewis can't make us accept his conclusion that "unless I believe in God, I can't believe in thought: so I can never use thought to disbelieve in God."

3. Now I go on to the next big division. People who all believe in God can be divided according to the sort of God they believe in. There are two very different ideas on this subject. One of them is the idea that He is beyond good and evil. *We* call one thing good and another thing bad. But according to some people that's merely our human point of view. These people would say that the wiser you become the less you'd want to call anything good or bad, and the more clearly you'd see that everything is good in one way and bad in another, and that nothing could have been different. Consequently, these people think that long before you got anywhere near the divine point of view the distinction would have disappeared altogether. We call a

cancer bad, they'd say, because it kills a man; but you might just as well call a successful surgeon bad because he kills a cancer. It all depends on the point of view. The other and opposite idea is that God is quite definitely "good" or "righteous," a God who takes sides, who loves love and hates hatred, who wants us to behave in one way and not in another. The first of these views—the one that thinks God beyond good and evil—is called Pantheism. It was held by the great Prussian philosopher Hegel and, as far as I can understand them, by the Hindoos. The other view is held by Jews, Mohammedans, and Christians.

4. And with this big difference between Pantheism and the Christian idea of God, there usually goes another. Pantheists usually believe that God, so to speak, animates the universe as you animate your body: that the universe almost *is* God, so that if it didn't exist He wouldn't exist either, and anything you find in the universe is a part of God. The Christian idea is quite different. They think God *made* the universe—like a man making a picture or composing a tune. A painter isn't a picture, and he doesn't die if his picture is destroyed. You may say, "He's put a lot of himself into it," but that only means that all its beauty and interest has come out of his head. His skill isn't in the picture in the same way that it's in his head, or even in his hands. I expect you see how this difference between Pantheists and Christians hangs together with the other one. If you don't take the distinction between good and bad very seriously, then it's easy to say that anything you find in this world is a part of God. But, of course, if you think some things really bad, and God really good, then you can't talk like that. You must believe that God is separate from the world and that some of the things we see in it are contrary to His will. Confronted with a cancer or a slum the Pantheist can say, "If you could only see it from the divine point of view, you would realise that this also is God." The Christian replies, "Don't talk damned nonsense." For Christianity is a fighting religion. It thinks God made the world—that space and time, heat and cold, and all the colours and tastes, and all the animals and vegetables, are things that God "made up out of His head" as a man makes up a story. But it also thinks that a great many things have gone wrong with the world that God made and that God insists, and insists very loudly, on our putting them right again.

These paragraphs are similar to those we have seen in other, more successful, arguments. They are essentially exposition, and they present facts and observations that the sympathetic reader can agree with. It is true enough, for instance, that "Christianity is a fighting religion."

5. And, of course, that raises a very big question. If a good God made the world why has it gone wrong? And for many years I simply wouldn't listen to the Christian answers to this question, because I kept on feeling "whatever you say, and however clever your arguments are, isn't it much simpler and easier to say that the world was *not* made by any intelligent power? Aren't all your arguments simply a complicated attempt to avoid the obvious?" But then that threw me back into those difficulties about atheism which I spoke of a moment ago. And soon I saw another difficulty.

6. My argument against God was that the universe seemed so cruel and unjust. But how had I got this idea of *just* and *unjust?* A man doesn't call a line crooked unless he has some idea of a straight line. What was I comparing this universe with when I called it unjust? If the whole show was bad and senseless from A to Z, so to speak, why did I, who was supposed to be part of the show, find myself in such violent reaction against it? A man feels wet when he falls into water, because man isn't a water animal: a fish wouldn't feel wet. Of course I could have given up my idea of justice by saying it was nothing but a private idea of my own. But if I did that then my argument against God collapsed too—for the argument depended on saying that the world was really unjust, not that it just didn't happen to please my private fancies. Thus in the very act of trying to prove that God didn't exist—in other words, that the whole of reality was senseless—I found I was forced to assume that one part of reality—namely my idea of justice—was full of sense. Consequently atheism turns out to be too simple. If the whole universe has no meaning, we should never have found out that it has no meaning: just as if there were no light in the universe and therefore no creatures with eyes we should never know it was dark. *Dark* would be a word without meaning.

So ends the argument. Why may a reader find it peculiarly unconvincing?

One reason is that Lewis tends not to answer the questions he raises. He does not respond to: "If a good God made the world why has it gone wrong?" Or: "But how had I got this idea of *just* and *unjust?*" We have already seen that he tends to jump from premise to conclusion without proper development in between. And that he likes to employ the flashy imperfect metaphorical analogy. He answers his own question about the just and the unjust with: "A man doesn't call a line crooked unless he has some idea of a straight line." He seems almost unaware that the analogy is metaphorical. Such flaws in the argument are part of the same technique: to create assent in the reader not by leading him carefully from the top of an argument to its bottom—but by bombarding him with assertions supported by mere appearance of logic.

The main reason that this argument is unconvincing, however, is that Lewis does not (the reader may infer) here believe in the very process of argumentation. We have seen other writers take the process seriously in a variety of ways by employing certain techniques already discussed. Argumentation for such writers is something of a partnership with the reader. One feels that they are convincing themselves as they convince the reader. This is one reason why the "pacing" of an argument is so important; both parties need time at certain points to absorb the material and to agree on the logical connections.

But Lewis was convinced before he began. He knew the truth, and was certain of it; so the only problem was to make it go down the reader's throat as easily as possible. Thus the sugar-coating effect of those pleasant but false analogies. Lewis was too good a thinker to believe that they were good ones.

Looking at the argument as a whole, we may conclude that it represents a certain amount of bad faith on the writer's part. Lewis has a kind of contempt for the reader's gullibility. He is contemptuous of argument as process and so creates sham rhetoric. It is ironic that a great writer—and a great Christian—should do so. And in doing so violate the *reality principle*. Lewis does not seem to care what the real world might tell us. Religious experience is indeed real enough; it is part of our universe of thought and feeling. But Lewis does not appeal to it. He is satisfied, like Orwell's O'Brien, with the reality inside his skull. God might be better served.[8]

While searching for material for this essay, I inspected many arguments. Their relative success seemed to depend not upon formula, particularly as found in textbooks, but upon basic strategy, such as that of proper pacing. When arguments succeed, they tend to use common techniques which can be recognized and described. This fact suggests a useful method of generalizing about the art of composition that refuses to recognize false distinctions between, for example, *exposition* and *argument, technical writing* and *freshman rhetoric, report writing* and *literary criticism.* Such terms represent compositions which argue and persuade and thus are more alike than different.

Arguments tend to succeed—the qualification is necessary—when a writer looks at the world with a skeptical eye: the world as it is, not as he would like it to be. A genuine argument will customarily deal, implicitly and explicitly, with the nature of the thing, and this is one reason why clear and realistic definition has always been an important element of good rhetoric. Another test of success is that of "refutability." If there is no possibility of refutation—no chinks, holes, or flaws anywhere—the argument put forth is in all likelihood too "perfect." It may, for example, substitute textbook logic for probability. And probability, as the ancients recognized, is the essence of successful argument. Other issues may enter in: ethical proof, the techniques of invention, methods of organization, to mention only a few. But if an argument does not recognize the governing factor of *probable truth,* it may have a fatal weakness.

Postscript:
What Researchers Say,
What Teachers Do

In 1976-1977, Charlene and I took a sabbatical trip (18,000 miles by car) around the United States. We visited high school English departments and talked to teachers and administrators. The results of that trip were reported in *What's Happening to American English?* Later, we did a similar but shorter survey of freshman composition programs in universities.

When I was preparing pilot material for the sabbatical, I happened to ask a university scholar and administrator in composition to identify a research study or type of study which had changed the way his university taught composition. "In other words," I asked, "what has made a difference?"

I got a long oral essay in response, but essentially his answer was: *Nothing has significantly changed the way we teach.* This intrigued me. I wanted to put my question into our questionnaire for the sabbatical study, but it was already mimeographed. So on our travels during and after the sabbatical I put the question, or something like it, to high school and college teachers and administrators. Sometimes I'd ask for a reaction to a specific scholar, subject, or technique: "Do you use Kinneavy's ideas in your comp. course?" "What aspects of classical rhetoric do you employ in teaching?" "What is the best device, in your department's opinion, for teaching figures of speech?"

The typical response to such questions surprised me then, and surprises me still. The high school teachers in our sample had never heard of Kinneavy, much less of his ideas. Classical rhetoric was dead in the universities. And figurative language was taught mainly as a matter of classifying tropes.

It has been a habit of mine to interview teachers and scholars informally about their work. Sometimes the teacher and scholar are the same person. The interviews are nothing fancy—ordinarily just a few questions about program, policy, teaching technique, textbooks, research and its applications, letting the conversation go where it will. Later, usually on the same day, I type up cards based on my notes.

In addition, I have been able to get an interesting sample of opinion on compositional matters from questionnaires returned from college teachers who have used the second and third editions of our textbook, *Strategies of Rhetoric*. In the opinions of these teachers I could detect a definite theme of hostility to ideas and practices based on contemporary research, even to those that are well and authoritatively established. For example, in opposition to authoritative opinion, teachers believe that the paragraph should be considered as a logical unit with a definite topic sentence; that sentences should be classified as simple, compound, and complex— and away with strange terms like *sentence opener;* that a subordinate clause must have subordinate meaning. And they want more grammar: "Expand the handbook"—even though it's already bloated.

One more story. Recently, I talked to some college teachers who work in one of the state sites affiliated with The National Writing Program (NWP), which has spread the benign influence of the Bay Area Writing Project over much of the United States. I asked them some of my favorite questions as we looked at a copy of the latest NWP brochure, which lists the "Assumptions" of the organization:

One: Change can best be accomplished by those who work in the schools, not by transient consultants who briefly appear, never to be seen again.

Two: Change agents in the schools should begin by focusing on what works.

Three: The best teacher of teachers is another teacher. Curriculum change cannot be accomplished with a packet of teacher-proof materials.

Four: Research and classroom practice have generated a substantial body of knowledge on the teaching of writing.

Five: A teacher of writing must write.

Six: The intuitions of teachers can be a productive guide for field based research, and practicing teachers can conduct useful studies in their classrooms.[1]

On the cover of the brochure, these words are quoted: ". . . teachers in the project are viewed as professionals, with their own areas of professional expertise, their own successful classroom experiences to report, and their own contribution to make to the improvement of their fellows. . . . This shared responsibility for improved teaching may be the theme of a new and exciting professionalism. . . ."[2]

I asked the NWP teachers: "What makes the Bay Area idea work so well?" They answered: "Teachers—teaching each other; teaching composition; writing and criticizing each other's writing —doing some things that before they just talked about in a classroom."

I said: "Would you tell me about some specific benefits of research, as *you* and other teachers see them. For example, do you employ any elements of the Christensen system?"

"No, hardly at all."

"Has Moffett or Macrorie or Donald Murray been of interest to you? Do you adapt their ideas for teaching?"

No, not in any formal way, they said.

I named other scholars. "What have they taught you?"

They shrugged.

I said: "NWP says here in its 'Assumptions' that 'Research and classroom practice have generated a substantial body of knowledge on the teaching of writing.'[3] But in effect you are telling me you don't use research in any consistent fashion. What about, say, sentence combining, which in sheer bulk of research, is very important now?"

One of the group, a woman, answered: "Some of our people teach a little sentence combining on their own, but we haven't found any broad applications for it."

"Then if it is not generally useful for you, as a part of the most successful nation-wide writing project in the country—perhaps in the history of the country—why are researchers spending so much time on it?"

"Ah," said a man, "because sentence combining is *researchable*. It's got a lot of problems you can put numbers to and fiddle with. It gives you an opportunity to interpret data and get results that look good quantitatively. But sentence combining as a major technique is more for publishing scholarly papers than for writing or teaching writing."

"Look at our Assumption Five," said another woman. "Our teachers *must write*. When they write, they don't use sentence combining. Why should they teach something they don't use themselves?"

My intent here of course is not to attack sentence combining, which strikes me as more sensible as a teaching device than certain other devices that have been touted recently. Rather, my intent is to throw light on a paradox. Modern theories in our field (and the techniques associated with them) tend to rise and fall like banana republics: one day all power and noise and glitter; the next day forgotten. What happened, for example, to the "new grammars"? Where are the transformationalists of yesteryear?

In 1968, that remarkable Harvard professor of language, Dwight Bolinger, wrote:

> If an applied linguist of the mid-1950s had gone to sleep in his cave, say around 1956, and awakened yesterday, the sight that greeted him would have sent him hurrying back to his dreams. Virtually every tenet that he had proclaimed in his heyday would have been returned to him upside down: writing once again beginning to assert itself over speech; grammar not learned inductively nor extended by analogy; language-learning not a matter of habit-formation; the goal of language-study to learn something about the human mind and not about linguistic behavior. And to cap this heap of insults, the poor fellow's descriptions of language were not very good and his claims to have anything to say to language teachers were not very well founded either.
>
> For those of us who could not enjoy the luxury of sleep while this clashing and reversing of gears was going on, the changes have meant some painful adjustments. For the teachers and the other people in the schools, who could not directly participate

but were only aware that what they had been led to regard as the anchor of their faith and works, its scientific basis, was beginning to give way, the effect was pure bewilderment.[4]

Perhaps what we are seeing as we enter the 1980s is the result of teachers' worlds being turned upside down once too often. Teachers of composition are no longer full of bewilderment, in Bolinger's phrase, about research. They are, to a great extent, simply ignoring it.

In the same week that I talked to the teachers in the National Writing Project, I read the essays in *Reinventing the Rhetorical Tradition.*[5] One interesting essay is by Edward P. J. Corbett, who talks at length about research on style. Professor Corbett lists the names you would expect to see: Christensen, Chomsky, Hunt, O'Hare, Daiker, Kerek, Morenberg, Shaughnessy, Ohmann, Hirsch, and others.

But when I talk to teachers across the country about what they do in classrooms and how they teach, such names are almost never mentioned. And if you look at their graded papers—I've seen hundreds of them—you find no particular evidence that these scholars and their findings ever existed. It is true that if you throw the name of Mina Shaughnessy into a conversation with teachers you will often get a reaction (in my experience, always a positive one). But if you ask how her ideas are adapted for specific classroom work—silence. Or, occasionally, "I haven't been able to work that out yet."

A publisher's reader saw an earlier draft of these remarks, along with a different version of the rest of the manuscript. The reader did not care much for the book, but he (or she) liked my postscript, in which I expressed a few doubts about research in composition. I obviously hit a nerve with the reader, who wrote: "I think [Tibbetts] is absolutely right about scientific research in composition; it is an opinion I have grown into in recent months while observing the prodigious efforts put into such work and the pitiful (laughable?) conclusions drawn from it." This reader suggested that I rebuild the book around that view: "I believe there's an audience eager to hear just such an opinion expressed. The whole book would benefit from a slightly more antagonistic tone . . . ."

But I don't want to be antagonistic to research and scholarship. I am in favor of them; how could a professor of composition not be?

My world would be much poorer without (for example) Professors Corbett, Christensen, and Hirsch—rather different scholars who have taught me much.

What I had tried to say in the earlier version, and am awkwardly trying to say now, is this. The scholar-researcher and the teacher of writing are pulling farther apart every day. If you judge by what he does in his daily work, the teacher no longer believes that researchers can give him valuable advice. The researchers can assert that this or another thing is true or useful, but so far as the teacher is concerned, little convincing evidence is presented to back up the assertion. And teachers won't read the scholarship carefully enough to learn certain genuine facts about composition—particularly those which tell us how successful writers think and act. If the scholar bears any blame, so should the teacher.

After reading the manuscript of this book, a scholarly friend of mine told me: "Your 'working papers' are good enough, but there's nothing new in them; your ideas are all in the literature somewhere." He is probably right. Yet I know from experience as teacher and administrator that, so far as writing performance is concerned, these ideas are new to almost everyone I teach or supervise, from college freshmen to second-year graduate students in English. *The ideas are in the literature but not in my students.*

This is an unfortunate situation.

Notes

Chapter One

1. E. D. Hirsch, Jr., *The Philosophy of Composition* (Chicago: University of Chicago Press, 1977), p. 9.
2. Mary P. Hiatt, *Artful Balance: The Parallel Structures of Style* (New York: Teachers College Press, Columbia University, 1975), p. 29.
3. *Ibid.*, p. 50.
4. Brand Blanshard, *On Philosophical Style* (Indiana University Press, 1967), pp. 55-57.
5. Sheridan Baker, *The Complete Stylist and Handbook*, 2d ed. (New York: Harper and Row, 1980), p. 16.
6. Quoted in John H. Dirckx, M.D., *Dx + Rx: A Physician's Guide to Medical Writing* (Boston: G. K. Hall and Co., 1977), pp. 50-51.
7. *Ibid.*, p. 52.
8. "The Fine Print Translated," *Time*, 22 September 1975, p. 74.
9. I first started working consciously with *sentence units* in 1957, while teaching remedial writing. But I didn't understand well what I was doing until I read Francis Christensen's *Notes Toward a New Rhetoric* (New York: Harper and Row, 1967).
10. Winston Churchill, "Leon Trotsky," *Great Contemporaries* (New York: G. P. Putnam's Sons, 1937), pp. 197-8.
11. Sir Cedric Hardwicke, *A Victorian in Orbit* (Garden City, New York: Doubleday and Co., 1961), p. 162.
12. I borrowed the last two bad sentences from Joseph Williams, "Defining Complexity," *College English*, 40 (February 1979), pp. 597, 601. The rewrites, however, are mine.
13. Hiatt, p. 39.
14. *Ibid.*, p. 40.
15. "Adjective Substitution Demonstration: Noun String Findings Analysis," *Fine Print*, No. 7 (May 1980), p. 1. In its eighth number, *Fine Print* changed its name to *Simply Stated*.

16. Bruce Price, "An Inquiry into Modifier Noun Proliferation," *Book World*, 12 April 1970, p. 8.
17. Nathaniel Shaler, *Autobiography* (Boston: Houghton Mifflin, 1909), pp. 98–99.
18. Wilfred Stone and J. G. Bell, *Prose Style: A Handbook for Writers* (New York: McGraw-Hill, 1972), p. 87.
19. Material on the Gunning-Mueller formula appeared in William E. Blundell, "Confused, Overstuffed Corporate Writing Often Costs Firms Much Time—And Money," *The Wall Street Journal*, 28 August 1980.
20. *Fine Print*, No. 5 (March 1980), p. 2.
21. Richard Weaver, *The Ethics of Rhetoric*, Gateway Ed. (Chicago: Henry Regnery, 1965), p. 116.

Chapter Two

1. Mark Twain, *Autobiography*, vol. 1 (New York: Harper and Brothers, 1924), p. 173.
2. Thomas Pyles, "English Usage: The Views of the Literati," *College English*, 28 (1967), pp. 443–54.
3. Lindley Murray, *English Grammar* (Albany: Hosford, 1819), p. 62.
4. For an extended account of these debates, see James Sledd and Wilma Ebbitt, eds., *Dictionaries and THAT Dictionary* (Glenview, Ill.: Scott, Foresman and Co., 1962).
5. Sir Ernest Gowers, *Plain Words: Their ABC* (New York: Knopf, 1962), p. 227.
6. John E. Warriner and Francis Griffith, *English Grammar and Composition* (New York: Harcourt Brace Jovanovich, 1977), p. 210.
   It is now a quarter-century since James Sledd published his paper in CCC *Journal* showing that subordinate clauses are not necessarily subordinate in meaning. See Sledd's "Coordination (Faulty) and Subordination (Upside-Down)," reprinted in *Applied English Linguistics*, ed. Harold Allen (New York: Appleton-Century-Crofts, 1958), pp. 354–362.
7. Gowers, p. 3.
8. This is the "avoidance technique" as given in the paperback version of A. M. and Charlene Tibbetts, *Strategies of Rhetoric* (Glenview, Ill.: Scott, Foresman and Co., 1979), p. 336.
9. Quoted in G. M. Wood, *Suggestions to Authors of Papers Submitted for Publication by the U.S. Geological Survey* (Washington: U.S. Government Printing Office, 1935), p. 50.
10. Mary McCarthy, "General Macbeth," *Harper's*, 224 (June 1962), p. 37.
11. William Faulkner, "A Rose for Emily," *These Thirteen* (Jonathan Cape and Harrison Smith, 1931), pp. 172–3.
12. Brooks Atkinson, introd. *Walden and Other Writings of Henry David Thoreau* (New York: Modern Library, 1950), pp. xiii–xiv.

Chapter Three

1. Mark Twain, *The Innocents Abroad, Works,* Vol. 1 (New York: Harper and Brothers, 1929), pp. 173-4.
2. Wayne Booth, "The Rhetorical Stance," *Now Don't Try to Reason with Me* (Chicago: University of Chicago Press, 1970), pp. 25-33.
3. Norman Mailer, *Miami and the Siege of Chicago* (New York: World Publishing Company, 1968), p. 130.
4. From E. Royston Pike, ed., *"Golden Times": Human Documents of the Victorian Age* (New York: Frederick A. Praeger, 1967). p. 343.
5. Booth, pp. 25-26.
6. See Donald Lemen Clark, *Rhetoric in Greco-Roman Education* (New York: Columbia University Press, 1957), pp. 73, 228-250.
7. Edward P. J. Corbett, *Classical Rhetoric for the Modern Student* (Oxford: Oxford University Press, 1965), p. vii.
8. Arn and Charlene Tibbetts, *What's Happening to American English?* (New York: Scribner's, 1978), pp. 58-59.
9. F. Peter Woodford, "Sounder Thinking Through Clearer Writing," *Science,* 12 May 1967, pp. 743-4.

Chapter Four

1. William J. Brandt, *The Rhetoric of Argumentation* (Indianapolis: Bobbs-Merrill, 1970), p. 70.
2. Richard Braddock, "The Frequency and Placement of Topic Sentences in Expository Prose," *Research in the Teaching of English,* 8 (Winter 1974), pp. 287-302.
3. Stephen Leacock, *How to Write* (New York: Dodd, Mead and Co., 1943), pp. 74-75.
4. Herbert Read, *English Prose Style* (Boston: Beacon Press, 1952), p. 54.
5. Charlton Laird, *The Miracle of Language* (New York: World Publishing Company, 1953), pp. 225-226.
6. Read, p. 52.
7. Larry Cohen, "The New Audience: From Andy Hardy to Arlo Guthrie," *Saturday Review,* 27 December 1969, p. 11.
8. *Ibid.*
9. Jacques Barzun and Henry Graff, *The Modern Researcher* (New York: Harcourt, Brace and World, 1962), pp. 136-137.
10. *Ibid.,* p. 55.
11. F. L. Lucas, *Style* (New York: Collier Books, 1962), p. 72.
12. Moses Hadas, *Imperial Rome* (New York: Time-Life Books, 1965), pp. 79-81.
13. Brandt, p. 70.

Chapter Five

1. Stephen E. Toulmin, *The Uses of Argument* (Cambridge University Press, 1964), p. 11.
2. Joy Gould Boyum, *"Tango* Crosses a Film Frontier," *The Wall Street Journal,* 9 February 1973.
3. Mike Royko, "Brando's Role: A Boring Slob," *Chicago Daily News,* 2 May 1973.
4. George Orwell, *Nineteen Eighty-Four* (London: Secker and Warburg, 1951), pp. 256, 271.
5. From Lon Fuller, "The Case of the Speluncean Explorers," *Harvard Law Review,* 62 (1949), p. 645.
6. *Ibid.*
7. C. S. Lewis, "What Christians Believe," *The Case for Christianity* (New York: Macmillan Co., 1947), pp. 31–35. The argument I have quoted is the first complete talk in a series of broadcasts later printed in both England and America.
8. Lewis is a favorite writer of mine, and I am sorry to disapprove of his work. However, this work of his, it seems to me, requires disapproval. Since an argument is a made thing, we can and should respond to the quality of its manufacture and materials. Prejudice or predilection need not play a major role in judgment. A Democrat should be able to recognize and judge a good argument made by a Republican; a pro-abortionist, a bad argument made by a fellow believer.

Postscript

1. Brochure of the National Writing Project, undated, unpaged. Disseminated at the national meeting of National Council of Teachers of English, November 1980.
2. Originally from an editorial, Ben Nelms, ed., *English Education,* (Spring 1979), National Council of Teachers of English.
3. NWP brochure.
4. Dwight Bolinger, "The Theorist and the Language Teacher," *Foreign Language Annals,* vol. 2, no. 1 (1968), p. 30.
5. Aviva Freedman and Ian Pringle, eds., *Reinventing the Rhetorical Tradition* (Conway, Ark.: University of Central Arkansas, L and S Books, 1980). Published for the Canadian Council of Teachers of English.